The Dating Game

Herbert J. Miles

ZONDERVAN
PUBLISHING HOUSE

OF THE ZONDERVAN CORPORATION | GRAND RAPIDS, MICHIGAN 49506

Dedicated
with affection and appreciation
to
our son and daughter-in-law
Stanley Wilson Miles
and
Linda Ballard Miles

Contents

Preface 11

1. THE NATURE OF COURTSHIP LOVE   15
   What is the difference between "like," "love," and
       "sex"? Can one draw a line between them?
   How can I know when I am in love?
   Is love at first sight possible?
   Seventeen and in love—an example

2. THE BEGINNINGS OF COURTSHIP   27
   What do teenage boys think about girls?
   What do teenage girls think about boys?
   At what age should first dating begin?
   Should a boy kiss a girl on the first date?
   What are some varied and creative courtship ac-
       tivities that will develop young people as per-
       sons, increase their interest in and devotion for
       each other, and help them to avoid dates that
       are routine and boring?

3. IN COURTSHIP WHO SHOULD DATE WHOM? . .   39
   What about marriage after dating only one person?
   Is there a "one and only"?
   Suppose two people want to court you and marry
       you. How do you decide between them?
   Should I marry "beautiful Betty" or "balanced
       Betty"?
   Is "dutch dating" socially acceptable?
   Wounded in courtship—an example

4. GOING STEADY 53

What is the relation of going steady to age?

What personal qualities should young people look for in selecting a marriage companion?

What qualities should young people avoid in selecting a marriage companion?

What are appropriate gifts to give during the going-steady period?

When your sweetheart drifts from you— an example

5. YOUR PARENTS AND YOUR COURTSHIP 65

How should teenagers handle parent-child conflict?

Why do parents worry about their children's courtship?

Should a young person insist on courtship and marriage when his parents strongly object?

How can young people develop a healthy independence from parents and at the same time develop a healthy, warm, and close personal relationship with them?

The dating problems of a seventeen-year-old girl —an example

6. ENGAGEMENT 77

What is the best procedure for a couple to follow in getting into engagement?

What are the things that a couple ought to do, discuss, and plan together during the engagement period other than planning the wedding ceremony and honeymoon?

Is it advisable for a girl to marry a college student who has several years of college and graduate work ahead, knowing he would be dependent on her for financial support?

As the date of marriage approaches, is the feeling

of doubt about choosing the right person very common?

How does one break an engagement?

How does one recover from a broken engagement?

When an engagement is broken, what is the proper procedure for returning gifts?

Some engagement danger signals—an example

7. SPECIAL PROBLEMS RELATED TO COURTSHIP, ENGAGEMENT, AND MARRIAGE 95

Must the boy be older than the girl in courtship and marriage?

Lovemaking in public?

What should be the attitude of the flat-chested girl as compared to a 36-24-36?

Is there a risk involved in marrying a person with a few minor bad habits?

Should courting couples confess past "skeletons in the closet" to one another before going to the marriage altar? If so, when?

What are the problems involved in marriage before or at the time of high school graduation?

Should parents help support their married children financially?

How does obesity affect courtship?

How can young people who think they are ugly keep their problem from blocking normal courtship?

8. THE PROS AND CONS OF SEX DURING COURTSHIP 117

How should young people respond to the current sex revolution?

What are the biblical teachings about sex?

Does the Bible discuss premarital sex?

Do churches equate sex with sin?

Is sex natural, like breathing, eating, and sleeping?

What are the social objections to premarital sex?

What are some of the arguments used in favor of premarital sex?

What about sex during engagement?

Should a single girl take the "pill" to avoid pregnancy?

What causes male sexual impotence?

What are the facts about Kinsey's study of female sex life?

9. PLANNING THE WEDDING CEREMONY 145

What about a secret marriage?

What is the financial cost of formal church weddings?

What are some ways to cut the cost of formal church weddings?

Should the wedding ceremony be built around the bride?

What about a marriage without a license or a wedding ceremony?

A suggested wedding ceremony, by Rev. Charles C. Hobbs

10. PLANNING THE HONEYMOON 161

How does a girl who is afraid of the physical side of marriage prepare for a honeymoon?

Should every first marriage be followed by a honeymoon?

Bibliography 167

Preface

What are the four most important decisions young people must make in planning their future? Most young people would agree that they are as follows:

1. Their choice of religious, moral, and social beliefs and values.
2. Their choice of a life's marriage companion.
3. Their choice of a life's vocation.
4. Their choice of how much education they should have.

Our culture has thousands of Christian churches that have majored in leading young people to commit their lives to Christ, through the processes of repentance and faith. We have countless vocational schools and counselors organized to assist young people in selecting a vocation. In recent years we have insisted that our young people get at least a college education. But our society has given little organized help to young people in going through the significant process of selecting a marriage partner. When Ernest G. Groves taught one of the first academic courses in marriage and the family at the University of North Carolina in 1927, many educators criticized it as being beneath the dignity of intellectual pursuits. Some still think such courses nonacademic and unnecessary. Thus the subject of courtship often has been left up to youthful trial-and-error methods influenced by the propaganda media and vested interests.

In truth, it is difficult for young people to separate these four life choices. They are all interrelated, and wise decisions are necessary in all of them to produce a balanced fruitful life of self-fulfillment.

Forty years ago young people began dating at the ages of fifteen to sixteen. Today, on the average, they begin at the ages of fourteen to fifteen. Many begin much earlier. Today the average girl marries at approximately age twenty to twenty-one, while the average boy at twenty-two to twenty-three. Boys and girls begin dating on the average at the same age (the girls are slightly younger). This means that the formal courtship process spans approximately six years for girls and eight years for boys. *These are important years.* If we will allow the major and acute problems of modern marriage and family life to flood our minds for a moment, it will become obvious that our young people need some organized help in the courtship processes. They not only need help, they want help, they welcome it. The purpose of this book is to give young people some positive help by discussing *sixty* of the major questions they are asking about the courtship processes.

The questions discussed in this volume come largely from *four* sources out of my life experience:

1. Teaching college marriage and family classes for twenty-three years.
2. Youth discussion groups in colleges and churches on problems related to courtship.
3. Experience in courtship and marriage counseling for twenty years.
4. Letters received from readers of my column "Courtship, Marriage, and the Family" that is now being published weekly in twenty-eight weekly and small daily newspapers in the Southeast.

The book is built around the six major courtship areas: (1) casual dating, (2) going steady, (3) engaged-to-be-engaged, (4) engagement, (5) the wedding, and (6) the honeymoon. Other topics that are closely related to courtship, such as age, parents, special problems, and the pros and cons of sex, are included.

The Dating Game is a Christian approach to courtship. It seeks to present a "middle-of-the-road" understanding of boy-girl relationships. When two extremes of a courtship problem are presented, often the discussion will echo the feeling that "there ought to be a middle ground." Then a middle-of-the-road approach is discussed and recommended.

I gratefully acknowledge my indebtedness to dozens of people who have made many contributions to the writing of this volume. I am deeply indebted to Charles C. Hobbs, college professor of English and the father of two teenagers, who has read the entire manuscript and made many valuable suggestions. I am grateful for his permission to publish in chapter 9 the ceremony he often uses in officiating at weddings. I am grateful to Judson T. and Mary G. Landis, Paul Popenoe, Henry A. Bowman, Evelyn Millis Duvall, and David R. Mace, who for the past four decades have been sociological pioneers in the areas of courtship, marriage, and the family as teachers, authors, lecturers, and counselors by systematically balancing scientific facts with tested social principles and values. Their contribution to the stability of family life has been a continual inspiration to me. I am also indebted to the following college students for their valuable guidance: George Ellis, Brenda Ellis, Lois Walker Miller, Ruby W. Flynn, Claudia Mann McKenzie, Rai Ette Williams, Sandi Chauncey, Stella Bumgardner, Sandra Beeler, Sheila Rowland Taylor, Oliver Chukwu, Marie Menindez, Judith Reeves, R. N. Lawson, Judy Rains, Joyce Holbrook, and Nancy Eby Hastings. They all worked diligently with me as student advisers, and made frank, practical, and intelligent suggestions. I am exceedingly grateful to Diane Yates who typed the manuscript from the first draft through its various stages to its final form.

1

The Nature of Courtship Love

Hello, young lovers! Early teens, middle teens, late teens, young adults, whoever you are, I admire you. I know how you feel. I am acquainted with your inner longings, your long-range purposes, and your secret dreams.

I want to encourage you to continue your interest in courtship. Do not be discouraged or defeated by trifles. You see, along the way there will be valleys and mountains. There will be clouds and rainbows. There will be storms and there will be peace.

Sometimes in your courtship you will be on the mountain top. You will seem to walk with wings. You will enjoy an "enchanted evening" together. Happiness will overflow. Yet, you may wonder, *Will I have sunshine day after day?*

Or, sometimes, after broken courtships, you may tread lonesome valleys and wonder, *What happened? What is wrong with me?* A storm will hide distant mountains and rainbows. You may feel discouraged about ever trying again. You may wonder, *Will there be no bright tomorrows?*

Young lovers, I once followed the happy courtship pathway that you are now traveling. I once played the roles of the game of courtship that you are now playing. Let's call this pathway and these roles *The Dating Game.* At age twenty-two I heard a lovely girl sing at a banquet. Her beautiful coloratura voice filled the banquet hall, crowded with community friends, neighbors, and local celebrities.

She sang a simple love song. In fantasy I thought—I hoped —she was singing to me. Yet I had never met her. After the banquet was over, I purposefully and hopefully went to compliment her and to get acquainted. I told her my name and complimented her on her singing. She smiled and spoke warmly to me, saying, "Thank you! I know about you. I have been hearing nice things about you." Her pleasant and welcome response caused my heart to pound. I wondered, *Could she be the one?* I hoped so. In a few weeks I asked her to be my guest at another banquet. Her response was again kind and affirmative. That banquet was a happy occasion with small, mutual initiatives and small, mutual, positive responses between us.

Many dates followed during the next two years. We walked and talked. Our voices rang with laughter. We clasped our hands and hearts. Hope, love, and bright tomorrows appeared. We planned, and planned, and dreamed. Often we prayed together. There were many warm embraces and tender kisses, with mutual understanding and mutual limitations. And then came a not unexpected proposal and a positive response. Following the engagement, a diamond! More plans, dreams, values, motives, and goals were crystallized and finalized. After two years, our dating game was crowned with a sacred wedding.

My memories of those happy days are rich just now. If I had it to do over again, I would do nothing differently, except that I would appreciate more and enjoy even more the happiness and blessings of "the dating game."

As it was for me, so the dating game should be to all young people everywhere: challenging! fun! crucial! It is divine plan and reality come alive and experienced by direct personal participation.

And so, young lovers, I have had a sweetheart, a lover, a love of my own, a love like yours. Therefore, let us reason together. Let's talk about you! Let's talk about love, the nature of courtship love! Let's talk about *your dating game*. May your rainbows drive your clouds away! May your mountains clasp hands and be joyful together!

When I was a teenage boy on a north-central Missouri farm, I saved my money and bought a Barlow knife. It had a sharp cutting edge. I was proud of my knife. Every farm boy owned and carried a knife, and we would often compare and sometimes trade them. We used them for many useful purposes. Across the weeks and months I used, misused, and abused my knife in cutting anything and everything until the sharp edge was so dull, blunt, and round that it would not cut anything.

The meaning of the word "love" as related to courtship is sharp and beautiful. But, like my knife, we have so misused and abused the word love with so many different meanings for so long that most young people are confused as to its real meaning. They have been taught that people should love God, parents, brothers and sisters, neighbors, sweetheart, husband or wife, foreign peoples, enemies, animals, and food. Psychology books tell young people to love themselves. The word love has been used to refer to childhood crushes and early teen infatuations. It has been used as a synonym of "sex." Thus the word love has been so abused for so long that puzzled young people are asking, "What is the real nature of the kind of courtship love that is a necessary prerequisite to entering a successful marriage?"

This is an intelligent question, an exceedingly practical question. To answer it is difficult, yet answer it we must. It is not necessary, here, to go into a heavy theological and philosophical discussion of the nature of love. Yet the reality of courtship love between a boy and a girl necessary for entering marriage needs to be stated in simple, practical language. This I propose to do.

WHAT IS THE DIFFERENCE BETWEEN "LIKE," "LOVE," AND "SEX"? CAN ONE DRAW A LINE BETWEEN THEM?

There is a difference between "like," "love," and "sex,"

and you can draw a line between them, but it is not easy. However, let's try it.

First, let us compare "like" and "love." Both animals and persons can like, but only persons can love. A dog likes food. As persons, we can like food, clothing, dogs, money, real estate, and things. We love only persons. We can like many persons, but you can really love (in the true courtship sense) only one person at a time. One can love parents and brothers and sisters. Love for them and for one's sweetheart has many elements in common. But there is a major difference between those elements. A young man's love for his sweetheart includes a sex interest and the possibility of a permanent "one-flesh" sex union through marriage.

Now, let us compare "sex" and "love." Both persons and animals possess sexual capacity. With animals, we can say that sex involves pleasure. We could say that animals enjoy sex. However, sex in animals operates on the level of biological instinct. It is generally not directed by love, concern, rationality, companionship, altruism, or any type of discrimination. These are human faculties that operate in human relationships in culture or society.

The human bodily aspect of sex is basically physical (biochemistry, physiology, biology) involving the muscular and circulatory systems (blood and blood vessels). It is a chemical process of the body. If not controlled, it is not rational. It is impersonal. It seeks its own. It is concerned only with the present. It operates without regard for others. Raw physical sex in human beings is greedy and "animallike."

However, persons are not just physical beings. We were created in the "image of God" (Genesis 1:27); that is, we were created mental-emotional-spiritual beings with the power of choice between right and wrong. We possess will, intellect, feelings, and motives. Thus, persons have the capacity to "love." We are twofold creatures. Let us say that a man or a woman is a unit, a total person composed of mind and body, of the physical and the nonphysical. Both the physical and the nonphysical work together as a total personal unit. Whereas sex is basically physical, love is basically mental-emotional-spiritual. Love involves the intellect, the will, the emotions. In courtship, human love is an interpersonal relationship between two persons of the opposite sex. It gives instead of receiving. It "seeketh not its own." It has deep concern for the one loved. The well-being of one's lover matters more to him than his own well-being. Courtship love is discriminating. A young man can like many girls, but he can love only one at a time.

In the plan of our Creator, love and sex operate together, beautifully. The nature of courtship love calls for the possibility of complete union, including sexual union in marriage. Beginning in courtship, love is concerned about the future. Thus, refraining from sex until marriage is evidence of love.

Persons can have sex relations without love. They can have sex relations with a person they do not even like. Dr. John W. Drakeford points out that "studies of college men's relationships with prostitutes show that while prior to the encounter they may have eagerly sought the experience, they were just as anxious to get away from the scene of the rendezvous, and refused to recognize the girls when they met on the street."[1] On the other hand, Dr. Drakeford points out that "love at its best is a growing deepening experience persevering through life. While sexual intercourse may take a few minutes to one hour, love has a continuing interest."[2] My research indicates that sexual intercourse during the first two years of marriage involves one of every eighty hours. However, the other seventy-nine hours are much more important to the couple. To quote Dr. Drakeford again, "Love is a complex totality, with sex but a part of a love experience."[3] The river of

---

[1] John W. Drakeford, *The Great Sex Swindle* (Nashville: Broadman, 1966), p. 91.

[2] Ibid.

[3] Ibid. p. 93.

human love flows both when the waters are calm and deep, and when the waters flow over the rocky riffles. When a boy and girl love each other, they both want to give the total sum of themselves to the satisfaction and happiness of the other. In doing this, in marriage, barriers of isolation and loneliness are broken down, but the individuality and personality of both are retained.

HOW CAN I KNOW WHEN I AM IN LOVE?

In the courtship processes, from puberty until marriage, all young people ask this question sooner or later. There is no thermometer, slide rule, or any kind of set formula that young people may use on themselves to decide absolutely that they are in love. A practical answer to the question must be idealistic.

If a person in courtship possesses the love necessary for a good marriage, certain attitudes, feelings, conditions, and circumstances should be present. Let us list some of them. If you are in love with a person most of the following conditions should prevail.

1. You will be concerned about your physical appearance (dress and grooming) and your personal conduct. One day a boy said to me, "Every time I am with her, she inspires me to be a better person."

2. You will have faith and trust in that person. In true courtship love a two-way fidelity and trust will always be present. They are Siamese twins that cannot be separated.

3. You will really not have a desire to date other people. Those whom you once thought you loved will recede into the background and into insignificance. Love, necessary for marriage, should be pure, confident, thorough, total, and complete.

4. You will want to see, to meet, and to know this person's parents, brothers, sisters, relatives, and friends. You will be anxious to please them. You will be concerned about the well-being of those near and dear to the one you love.

5. You will delight in the personal accomplishments of the person you love. You will not be jealous of that person's achievements. Of course, if a third party approaches your sweetheart, with courtship in mind, you will be jealous. Love is like that! This is a natural, normal jealousy! But you will not be jealous of your lover's characteristics and potentialities. You will delight and rejoice in the accomplishments of the person you love, even though some of these may be superior to your own.

6. You will have respect for the one you love. You will respect that person's beliefs, values, moral standards, rights, and needs. You will respect that person as a person, a total person.

7. You will have a feeling of inner security as a result of your love for this person. You will feel self-confident, relaxed, and happy even in the face of major personal, social, or financial problems.

8. You will be lonely when circumstances force you to be separated. It will be difficult for you to keep your thoughts and dreams off your lover. You will long for the day and hour when you can be together again.

9. You will sacrifice for the person you love in many different ways. You will enjoy bringing gifts to that person. Love is an outgoing something. It is possible for a person to give without loving, but it is impossible to love without giving! "God so loved the world that he gave. . . ." This is the nature of love!

10. You will be hurt when your sweetheart is hurt or criticized. You will rush to the defense of your lover. This is not a case of "my sweetheart, right or wrong." (Love must be guided by rational, intelligent reality.) But rather, it is an illustration of the nature of love. Love automatically responds to the needs and protection of the one loved.

11. You will want this person to become, in marriage, the father or mother of your children. You will want your children to have the character, qualities, and attitudes of your sweetheart.

12. You can honestly say that your interest in this person

is not simply a physical attraction, a sexual interest, but rather, your interest is in the total person, as a complete personality, involving every aspect of life. To be sure, to be in love with a person includes physical attraction and sexual interest in marriage. This is a major aspect of love. But if it is the only interest between a couple, it is not love! It is lust! And certainly the sexual interest must never be the first interest. Sex is a part of true love, but it is the servant of all other personal and personality relationships.

13. Other people will know that you are in love. It is nearly impossible for a person in love to keep it a secret. You will bubble over with happiness. Your relatives and friends will suspect it. They will know it. They will tell you so.

These conditions do not happen in a minute or by blind accident. They are the result of a careful process of intelligent association, thinking, planning, dialogue, prayer, and divine leadership (cf. John 6:38). Those who scoff at the idealism of this discussion should recall the attitudes, feelings, and behavior of their own courtship days and then read this discussion again. It may help them to be more understanding of their children who are going through the courtship years.

IS LOVE AT FIRST SIGHT POSSIBLE?

Many fine young people and adults claim to have experienced love at first sight. Some who claim love at first sight in the early and middle teens never marry the one they were "in love" with. Their experience may be labeled "infatuation" or "an emotional response." Or they might simply be in love with the idea of love. It is not difficult to understand why some believe in love at first sight. Young people have been persistently bombarded (by romantic literature, movies, the propaganda media, and pulp magazines) with the idea that love at first sight is the beginning of courtship.

Many writers concerned with marriage and the family have come to describe this bombardment by what they call "bogus romance." It includes three steps. (1) Boy meets girl and both are suddenly gripped by a strange inner feeling (love at first sight). (2) They immediately leave everything and everybody for this new feeling (they commit marriage). (3) Six months later this sudden and strange feeling has just as suddenly and strangely gone (they commit divorce and start over). This cannot be love. It sounds more like a deep and intense case of stupidity.

What actually happens in the encounter of a couple who insist they have experienced love at first sight? Young people from the middle teens until marriage give much thought to possible marriage and the type of person they want to marry, and rightly so. A mental image of this future person is formed. This image may include physical traits and nonphysical traits, such as education, religion, morals, values, or ambition. Let us imagine that one day, by chance, Fred and Ruby come in contact with each other. At first sight, she is beautiful. He is handsome. They maneuver an introduction. In this process the mental image of the person they want to marry floods each mind. This image is read into the strange new friend. The proverbial "butterflies in the stomach" begin to flutter. They each welcome and pursue the conversation with smiles, kindness, and "left-handed"compliments. Fred later calls Ruby for a date. They date regularly, and later they begin to go steady. Across the weeks and months they find that they have values, goals, ambitions, ideals, and many other things in common. They become engaged and are married.

During the courtship and marriage they insist it was "love at first sight." Was it? Let us go back to the day they first met. Honestly now, what really happened? Was it love at first sight? *No!* It was physical attraction at first sight, including sexual attraction. It is normal for young people to be attracted to each other, physically. Not to be would be abnormal. In courtship there has to be a "starting place," and the normal starting place is physical attraction. But do we have a right to call *this* "love at first sight"? When Fred and Ruby saw each other for the first time, they were attracted physically and the "butterflies flew." But, they knew *nothing* about each other except that they were physically attracted and may have had some lightning-fast dreams about the future. Why don't we all be frank about the process of getting into love? It takes weeks, or months, or sometimes years for real love to grow and develop until the Freds and Rubys are certain "this is it." In other words, getting into love is a process, not a single act. It takes time, association, cooperation, initiatives, and responses to develop love. Love *is* a reality! One has to work to develop it! Love can wax and wane. One can gain it; one can lose it. One has to work hard to keep it! And really, it is not something achieved; it is something each gives.

SEVENTEEN AND IN LOVE—AN EXAMPLE

Recently I received a letter from a typical seventeen-year-old boy asking my opinion about his courtship relationship with his new sweetheart. His letter and my response to it serve as an example of how young people can apply the nature of courtship love to their own specific courtship experience. Here is his letter:

> I don't have a problem, but I would like your opinion on my situation. Three weeks ago my family and I went on a vacation to another state to visit some of our relatives. My cousin is going with a girl there, and she has a friend, Helen, with whom I fell in love. We both really do love each other a lot. We call each other all the time and write letters to each other every night. We hope to have big plans in the near future. I just turned seventeen, and I am a sophomore in high school. I am sure everything will work out between us. We don't have any problems with each other because we both really love each other. Do you think this is a good thing or not, since she lives 250 miles away from me? I know Helen's not stepping out on me with other boys. Please give me your advice. How

should I handle this? It really means a lot to me. Thank you.
A teenager in love,
Tom.

Tom wrote an honest letter expressing the truth about his present feelings toward his new sweetheart. What he asked is (1) Is this a good relationship? (2) Can it survive? (3) How should I handle it? He is to be congratulated for seeking advice. This is an act of wisdom. He wanted an honest and factual answer.

Tom's relationship with Helen is a good thing; that is, it can be if they handle it properly. It is normal for a boy his age to be interested in girls and in the possibility of future marriage. I would be worried about him if he were not. Normal young people may have five or six (or more) "crushes" on different members of the opposite sex in the process of growing up.

There are a few things that trouble me about Tom's letter. He is sure they are both "in *love*," and they have known each other only three weeks. Would it not be better at this point to say that they *like* each other very much? This is much too soon to have developed mature love. It is certainly possible that, in the future, Tom and Helen may develop mature love for each other. Also, his letter indicated that he "fell in love at first sight." As already stated, getting into love is not "an act" but a "process" that develops over an extended period of time. When Tom talks about "big plans in the near future," does he mean engagement and possible marriage? On the average, young men in our society get married at the age of twenty-two and one-half years. Counting his seventeenth year, he still has six and one-half years before he reaches the average marriage age. In the meantime, they would have to have a long engagement or marry as teenagers. Either can present major problems.

Can Tom's relationship with Helen survive? Yes! This is possible, if they both handle their future relationships properly. However, judging the two by the past experiences of thousands of other fine young people, the chances are much greater that it will not succeed than that it will. The 250-mile separation presents a problem, but it is not insurmountable.

How should Tom handle this? I suggested that they both should consider the following ideas: They should continue their interest in each other, writing often. If possible, they might plan to visit one another two or three times a year until they are through high school. When they are together, they should enjoy one another, carefully avoiding familiar intimacies that will tempt them both beyond their will power. A gentleman protects a girl, he does not violate her.[4] They should be active in programs of their high school classes. They should prepare for some kind of responsible occupation or profession that will stabilize their future marriage. Through letter writing, they should develop a sound Christian life philosophy, including Christian morality and values. They should not consider themselves as going steady at this point. Both ought to date some other people. By the time they are nineteen they should have dated a dozen different people. This will help them to understand a variety of personalities, attitudes, and problems of the opposite sex and will help them to make the right decision about each other.

I suggested that both Tom and Helen show my reply to their parents. They should discuss their future interests in one another with them in detail. Their parents should listen and reason with them, and they with their parents.

Tom is no longer a child. He is not yet a man. He is in-between. Love is a mature emotion! Marriage is for mature adults! The next few years for Tom and Helen are very important! They should plan and live them well! The teen years should be responsible years, years of growth. Yet they should be years of happiness and fun. Young people should not hurry through them.

---

[4] I suggested that they secure and read a copy of my book *Sexual Understanding Before Marriage*, 1971 (Zondervan Publishing House, 1415 Lake Drive, S.E., Grand Rapids, Mich., 49506, paperback $1.95).

2

The Beginnings of Courtship

WHAT DO TEENAGE BOYS THINK ABOUT GIRLS?

On this question a fifteen-year-old girl wrote me as follows:

> What do boys between the ages of thirteen and eigh-
> teen like, dislike, and/or want out of girls? Do they like to
> be around old-fashioned girls, decent girls, or forward girls,
> or do they like to be around girls at all? What do they
> really expect from us? I would like to know what goes on
> in their heads about us.

Let us describe briefly the social situation and psychological feelings of boys from age thirteen to eighteen. They
reach puberty at age thirteen to fourteen. (More precisely,
it is an average of 13.3. Legally, it is considered 14.) Puberty
is the age at which a boy's reproductive system begins
to produce sperm cells. He undergoes major changes in
height and in attitudes. Life begins to take on new meanings. He is not allowed to drive a car until sixteen. He
cannot vote until eighteen. He is in a sort of "twilight
zone" between childhood and adulthood. He is not sure
of himself. He is uncertain and lacks self-confidence. He
does not like to admit this to himself or to others. He is
not sure about the nature of his body, his sexual nature,
his ideas about girls, his ideas about life. He is searching
for identity; that is, "What is my nature?" "What should
I believe about life?" and "What should I do in life?" Or,
to state it another way, "What is God's plan and will for

my life?" "What does society expect out of me?" and "How can I fit these two together?" Boys should not be ashamed of these facts. Rather, they should be happy, proud, and challenged that they are in the process of entering manhood. This life period is as natural for them as it is for "sparks to fly upward." Girls (and everybody else) should understand boys in light of this "growth twilight zone."

Now, what do these boys like, dislike, and expect from girls? We may be sure that, secretly, they like girls! At thirteen, they like to go to boy-girl parties, but, in their inexperience, they tend to stay together in groups and hesitate to show their inner interest in girls. At fourteen boys tend to lose interest in boy-girl relationships for a while. Some boys do not show interest again until they date during their senior year in high school. Others fall head-over-heels in love several times during the teen years. When they change sweethearts, it doesn't seem to hurt them, even if the girl initiates the break-up. Many boys age fifteen and sixteen like *group* boy-girl relationships. This fits into their uncertainty and inexperience. For the same reason, the early- and middle-teen boys like girls younger than they are. Some enjoy and feel comfortable in forming a close sort of "brother-sister" relationship with certain girls, if they can do so without being forced into individual dates. They will talk, be kind, and enjoy such companionship. But they will drop a brother-sister relationship if she gets "serious." Even when parents encourage boys age sixteen and seventeen to have individual dates with different girls, they generally do not, even though they would like to.

In general, middle-teen boys like girls and enjoy associating with them, but they are not ready to get serious. In the good sense, they like "old-fashioned" girls. They like "decent" girls and have plans to marry one. Only a selfish, fly-by-night "playboy" is interested in "indecent" girls. Boys like a "forward" girl in the sense that she talks, smiles, laughs, is kind, unselfish, radiant, and has an outgoing personality. They enjoy being around such a girl.

I suggest middle-teen girls plan some church or community meeting for recreation. It could be understood that girls may invite boys to meet them there. The party plan would be so organized that boys and girls would pair off for association. But it would not be an official, individual date. This opens the way for association which the boys want, but protects them from their fear of inexperience. Parents ought to be interested in helping their children in this type of recreation.

WHAT DO TEENAGE GIRLS THINK ABOUT BOYS?

It is true that teenage girls want to know what teenage boys think about them. It is *equally* true that teenage boys want to know what teenage girls think about *them*. In order to discuss this, let us reverse the first question and ask it as follows.

> **What do girls between the ages of thirteen and eighteen like, dislike, and/or want out of boys? Do they like to be around old-fashioned boys, decent boys, or forward boys, or do they like to be around boys at all? What do they really expect from them? Why do some girls tend to have periods of moodiness?**

Let me describe briefly the physical, social, and psychological situation and feelings of girls at the age of puberty. Girls reach puberty approximately at the age of twelve and a half years. Puberty is the time when a girl's ovaries begin to produce egg cells (ova). This marks the beginning of her monthly menstrual cycles.[1] At puberty a girl undergoes major changes in height and in attitudes. Life begins to take on new meanings. She reaches puberty on the average nearly one year ahead of boys. At puberty she becomes openly interested in boys. A girl who has reached puberty at eleven and a half years (some do much earlier) will

---

[1] For a detailed discussion of the menstrual cycle, see my book *Sexual Understanding Before Marriage* (Grand Rapids: Zondervan Publishing House, 1971), p. 44.

show interest in eleven-year-old boys who may be two years away from puberty. At that age the boys have little or no interest in girls. This places girls in an uncomfortable and embarrassing social and emotional situation. In this situation, it is an inexcusable mistake for parents to accuse their daughter of being "boy crazy." Parents need to understand her situation and help her to understand it. Girls should not be ashamed of physical and emotional changes that appear at puberty. Rather, they should be happy, proud, and challenged that they are in the process of entering womanhood.

Now, what do girls, age thirteen to eighteen, like, dislike, and expect from boys? We may be sure that girls like boys. They let it be known either openly or in sly, subtle ways. They like boys to be neat, clean, and well-groomed. They dislike boys who look more like barnyard animals or beasts of the field than human beings. They like boys who are honest, who can be depended upon to do what they say they will do. They want a boy to come by for them to go to the party at the time he said he would and not one-half hour later. They like boys who will help them carry on the conversation. They do not like a boy who spends all the time talking about himself. A girl likes a boy who is not jealous of her on a date to the point of being angry if she speaks to another boy. Girls just do not like boys who are too possessive.

They like boys who are decent boys. Yes, they like "old-fashioned" boys, boys who respect both the girl's moral ideals and her person. They like boys who are extroverts (when not too loud and excessive), who have fun, who tease, and who give honest compliments.

They like boys who can understand their feelings, emotions, and moods. Girls don't have a monopoly on having moods. However, many girls' feelings and attitudes can be influenced by a glandular disturbance in connection with her monthly period.

Two college seniors, Roger and Anne, were engaged to be married. Three months before their wedding date Roger came to my office. He had begun to doubt the wisdom of marriage. He said that Anne would be so moody sometimes on a date that it would be boring. Most of the time she was wonderful. But her occasional moods worried him. He wondered if these moods increase after marriage. I inquired if this might result from her premenstrual period. He did not seem to understand what I was talking about. I explained to him the premenstrual problems of some girls and suggested that since they were engaged, that he talk to Anne about it. The next day Roger came rushing into my office, elated. He said, "I have good news! Last night I searched my diary and found that Anne's moody periods showed up on the dot every twenty-eight days."

Girls like boys who look for their inner qualities. They like nonsmokers, nondrinkers, and non-drug users. They dislike boys who are materialistic, opinionated, egotistical, crude, or harsh. Let me assure all teenage boys: *Girls like boys!*

AT WHAT AGE SHOULD FIRST DATING BEGIN?

There are two kinds of age: calendar and maturity age. The latter is more important than the former. Young people vary. Some at thirteen are as mature as the average eighteen-year-old. Some eighteen-year-olds are less mature than the average thirteen-year-old. Yet, it is difficult to keep from thinking in terms of the calendar age.

Group parties sponsored by adults allow young people healthy association during the predating age. The group association, properly sponsored, is good. It may tend to delay too early individual dating.

Most parents do not want their children to date too early, not because they are old "fuddy-duddies" but because they are familiar with the possible consequences and dangers involved.

Most youth age twelve to fourteen are overanxious about dating. It is difficult for them to face the fact that maturing is a slow and gradual process. Most thirteen-year-old girls think they are more mature than the average and therefore should be allowed to date.

When youth age twelve to fourteen grow up, marry, and have children of their own, they will feel the same as their parents feel now toward them. They will love their children and want to guide them around the dangerous pitfalls involved in too early dating.

Solid sociological research indicates that the earlier dating begins, the younger the marriage age. It indicates further that the earlier the marriage age, the higher the divorce rate.

Some social-climbing parents "jump the gun" and allow their sons and daughters to date while mere children. Dr. Thomas Poffenberger, in a study of both junior high and senior high school students, found that 13 percent had had dates at age twelve years and under, and 19 percent had had dates at age thirteen. Also he found that 5 percent had "gone steady" at age twelve and under 9 percent had gone steady at age thirteen. Since on the average girls reach puberty at twelve and a half and boys at thirteen and a half, this means that a considerable number of his sample were dating and going steady before puberty.[2] I am sure that most mature, thinking youth age twelve and thirteen can see that dating before puberty is absurd, and the parents who allow it are irresponsible. Those misguided parents push young children out of childhood into adult activities and are causing them to miss the wonderful maturing periods of adolescence and youth. This causes personality and mental health problems.

On the other hand, some parents are authoritarian tyrants who refuse to allow their daughters to date until sixteen or seventeen or eighteen years of age. This is equally as absurd and irresponsible.

Fifty years ago the acceptable age for the first date was sixteen. Gradually the age for the first date is drifting lower.

---

[2] Judson T. Landis and Mary G. Landis, *Building a Successful Marriage*, 5th ed. (New York: Prentice-Hall, 1968), p. 47.

This drift has caused many parents to become alarmed. About ten years ago Dr. David Mace wrote an article in a national magazine in which he suggested that too-early dating was getting out of hand in the United States. He recommended that, since parents had not been able to cope with the problem, the National Congress should pass a law that American youth were not to have dates until age fifteen. The following short summary outlines his defense of the idea.

1. Too early dating promotes social tyranny. You either have a date, or you can't go to the party. If you don't find a partner, then you are a failure. This leads to insecurity and shyness in boys and girls.

2. Too early dating fosters a subtle form of mutual exploitation. Our cultural mores encourage the boy to go as far as he can sexually with his date. If he doesn't, he is a failure.

3. Too early dating becomes extremely expensive. Girls exploit boys financially. They expect expensive dates and expensive gifts. Boys under sixteen normally have earned very little money but are often required to spend large sums of money on one date in an evening. Girls also exploit their parents. They demand expensive dresses and often have to have a new one for each big occasion. So reasoned Dr. David Mace.[3]

I personally would not favor this law. Frankly, I do not think Dr. Mace expected it to become law. He was trying to force us to think about the dangers of too-early dating. He was saying that too-early dating intensifies social tyranny, sexual and financial exploitation.

It is normal for boys and girls to be interested in each other at ages thirteen and fourteen. If they were not, I would be worried about them. Young people in the early teens should be honest with themselves about their interest in the opposite sex. They should discuss the subject with their parents. They should have a talk with them

---

[3] *McCalls*, August, 1961, Volume 88, pp. 96, 97.

frequently. May I suggest a discussion in which someone reads a question and the discussion from this book and then follows through with a group discussion? It is a fact that both youth in their early teens and parents want to talk to each other about courtship, sexual development, and related topics and to help each to understand the other. Also young people should feel free to discuss these topics with their pastor, Sunday school teacher, or school guidance counselor. To do so will keep the lines of communication open.

SHOULD A BOY KISS A GIRL ON THE FIRST DATE?

There are two extreme attitudes concerning courtship kissing. In the past there have been those who said that kissing belonged only to marriage, and others have said that young people should not kiss until after a "genuine engagement." At the other extreme, some "moderns" advocate kissing on the first date, and encourage early teen dating. Both positions are very unrealistic. There ought to be a reasonable and acceptable middle ground.

It is not difficult to understand why today's youth advocate kissing on the first date. The adults in our society have taught them to do so through the propaganda mass media and the philosophy of the so-called "new morality." If we ask today's youth to explain why they advocate kissing on the first date they usually give one or more of the following replies: (1) It is natural, normal, and healthy. (2) Why not? Everybody does it! (3) If a boy is a gentleman during the date, he deserves a kiss. (4) If a boy has to pay out money on a date, he has a right to kiss his date if he wants to. (5) It is an expression of friendship. (6) It is simply expressing thanks for a good time. (7) It poses no greater problem than a normal "thank you" or a handshake.

It is obvious to mature, thinking young people that most of these explanations are questionable, small part-truths and deserve careful examination. Is kissing on the first date really harmless? Is it healthy mentally and emotionally? How many young men have kissed a girl on the first date, only to have her read a lot more into the kiss than he meant for her to? How many young men have lost some respect for the girl who was so eager to be kissed on the first date? How many young girls have felt the pang of regret after finding out that the first-date kiss meant nothing to *him*, because he never called for another date?

How many young people have argued with their parents, using that famous line "Everybody is doing it"? Is this statement really true? Honest now! Do not young people use this argument because they lack a real reason? Is this not empty argument to justify whatever we want to do? What would happen to human behavior if everybody flowed along with the shifting tides of "what everybody is doing"? For example, suppose almost everyone is following a new fad that calls for "swallowing a live goldfish" once every week; does this make it right? Are there not better ways for youth to decide what is right and what is wrong in boy-girl relationships than the weak statement "Everybody is doing it"?

If kissing is merely a way of expressing friendship, then why save it for dates? Are there not many other excellent ways of expressing friendship?

Do the arguments that the boy "has been a gentleman and deserves something for it" and that he "has paid out money on the date and has a right to a kiss" really ring true? Does this not lower the kiss to nothing more than a type of payment? Do girls really want to date boys who expect a price for every date? Isn't this immature childish exploitation?

If kissing good-night on the first date is just like a handshake or saying "thank you," why not shake hands and say, "Thank you for a lovely evening"?

More realistically, are not the motives behind kissing on the first date (1) social pressure, (2) fear of not getting other dates, and (3) the physical pleasure of the stimulation involved? Are not these motives rather immature, artificial, and counterfeit?

To argue against kissing on the first date is not to argue against all kissing in courtship. A middle ground, a positive approach to courtship kissing, should involve mature people who through association have developed mutual, mature love for each other. It should involve personal respect. It should be related to the proper time, the proper place, the proper understanding, and the proper restraint. It should never be an "end in itself," but always a means to other ends, namely, a further development of love and marriage plans. Instead of selfish exploitation and satisfaction, let us be grateful to Him who created us male and female and gave us the spiritual love, understanding, and fulfillment we receive. Tennyson, in "Locksley Hall," put it like this: "Our spirits rush . . . together at the touching of the lips."

WHAT ARE SOME VARIED AND CREATIVE COURTSHIP ACTIVITIES THAT WILL DEVELOP YOUNG PEOPLE AS PERSONS, INCREASE THEIR INTEREST IN AND DEVOTION FOR EACH OTHER, AND HELP THEM TO AVOID DATES THAT ARE ROUTINE AND BORING?

This question calls for a positive reply. For many years as a college professor I have been nauseated every time I hear some lazy person whine, "There isn't anything for young people to do." Recently when I was leading a youth group discussion on "courtship," a boy in the back who had said nothing, stood and said, "Why are you adults so narrowminded? You don't want us to drink, to smoke pot, to gamble, to pet, or to have premarital sex. What are young people to do?" His question falsely assumed that there was nothing else to do. There may have been a time in years past in some isolated areas that there was little organized recreation for youth. That day is past. The real problem of modern young people is not in finding something to do. The real problem is finding time to do the many wonderful, varied, creative things that can be done.

It is helpful to think of courtship activities in two groups: (1) spectator amusements, and (2) participation recreation. In spectator amusements, groups gather to watch others perform. The individual is often rather passive. Every week in every county in the United States there is a football, basketball, or baseball game. Often there are many of them. Every week in most every county there are recitals, concerts, lyceums, and lectures. Every day in every county there is some kind of movie. Every hour of every day in almost every home, radio and television entertainment is available. Too much of what goes on at the movie and on television is pitched on the level of low-grade morons. Most young people are high school and college graduates and will not be interested in filling their minds with such trivial garbage. To be fair, there are some selected programs coming over the media that are valuable scientifically, socially, morally, and spiritually.

In many areas there are excellent art and historical museums. And, of course, every boy should take his sweetheart one time to the circus and to the zoo.

I recommend that spectator amusement constitute a *small* percent of courtship dating (a minimum of 10 percent, a maximum of 25 percent). Thus, I am saying young people should want creative participation recreation in 75 to 90 percent of their dates. Recreation means to "re-create," that is, to restore, to refresh, and to strengthen your mind, body, and soul. Participation recreation includes tennis, golf, bowling, swimming, skating, bicycling, boating, skiing (water and snow), volleyball, handball, shuffleboard, badminton, ping pong, hiking, and mountain climbing, to name a few.

Other participation recreation may be planned at home, including an evening cooking a meal, making candy, popping corn, or enjoying a cook-out in the back yard. How about an evening with each set of parents where there is singing, music, or games? Or you might read aloud some books on youth problems, health, or other subjects that would stimulate mental growth. How about a date where both try to write a poem together? Why not antique a piece of furniture? How about collecting and repairing toys to be given to neglected children?

To be active in church life during your courtship can be very creative. Many churches have a recreation room and promote youth socials, sweetheart banquets, and youth-service projects. How about planning a progressive supper for the youth of your church? Space does not permit a listing of the many, many youth activities sponsored by our high schools and colleges that open the way for creative courtship activities.

A boy and his sweetheart could plan and direct a picnic for underprivileged children. Or they could enlist some other couples to go to the homes of some lonely people who are shut-in or sick. Everyone would introduce himself. Some songs, a devotional, and a prayer would be in order. After the visit a get-together at the ice-cream parlor should complete a pleasant evening for the group.

I have just started on the long, long list of possible varied creative activities available to youth during the courtship days. Who was it that said, "There isn't anything for young people to do"? Shame! Shame! The real problem is finding time and planning well those creative activities that develop dating youth as total persons and develop their interest in each other. In the beginning courtship days, it is good to observe each other in as many different situations and circumstances as possible. Creative ingenuity in recreational activities will destroy routine and boredom, and just possibly could lead to future engagement and a happy marriage.

3

In Courtship Who Should Date Whom?

WHAT ABOUT MARRIAGE AFTER DATING ONLY ONE PERSON?

Many young people are concerned about this question, and rightly so. This dating-only-one type of courtship often starts in dating too early and is promoted by habit. Could it be that insecurity and fear (of not finding someone else) feeds this habit? Before marriage, young people tend to see each other through rose-colored glasses. Their date is perfect mainly because they want him to be perfect. I suspect that many tend to look at each other's good traits and tend to ignore the bad ones. Anyone who ignores the bad traits of his sweetheart during courtship is playing with dynamite. In seeing only the good traits, one is running a high risk of building up an "ideal person" around his "ideal love." This is like building a straw house on the sand, and down the line when the "real person" emerges in marriage, the "ideal person" will collapse, often with great disillusionment and sorrow.

Before considering marriage, the couple must consider carefully, "How will we feel about each other after marriage when the 'real you' begins to emerge?" One or both may become demanding or possessive in an effort to repair and regain the "ideal person." Probably both need to learn that one person cannot be remade by another. Efforts to do so are usually sadly disappointing. After a mistake is made in marriage, it is too late to cry! It is usually very difficult to return "damaged merchandise." And it will be shocking to realize that two "strangers" are living together in marriage.

Two examples come tumbling into my mind. A young woman who was married three years came secretly to my office for a conference. She wanted to talk to me in professional confidence. She had never dated anyone but her husband, and they had been happy. "But recently," she said, "I have been being attracted to other men, and I am haunted by the idea that I made a mistake. I should have dated other people before I married."

In a similar manner, a young man who was married and had one child came for a conference. He said, "I dated only one girl, my childhood sweetheart, and married her. But now I remember another girl I used to like very much and had serious thoughts of dating her some, but I never did. The girl I married never knew of my interest in the other girl. Recently my wife and I met her at a social occasion. She is still single. I have been greatly disturbed since meeting her. Memories of my past concern for her have flooded and confused my thinking. The idea that I made a mistake in my courtship and marriage by never dating anyone else has fastened itself on my mind, and I can't shake it loose."

In order to avoid similar future problems, courtship and marriage need to be based on a mature evaluation of self and of others. This can best be done by dating many different persons in the early stages of courtship.

One of the greatest joys of marriage is being able to find special traits in your companion that you were unable to find in others. This is what makes the person special, and *yours!* How can you really know what type of person you want to marry if you do not know who else is available? By not dating anyone else, a young person is not qualified to evaluate his sweetheart, nor to evaluate his own personality.

However, to be objective, I must state that there are cases of successful marriage where one or both never dated anyone else. All of us have known a few such cases. They are certainly the exception and not the rule. They are the results of coincidence rather than wise planning. The risk is great, indeed! Be sure to shop around before you buy! Marriage is a big, big decision!

IS THERE A "ONE AND ONLY"?

The idea of a "one and only" in selecting a marriage partner is the belief that some infinite power or force outside of you, such as God or fate, selects in advance some one individual as a marriage partner for you. This one person has unique personality traits that fit your needs. You are passive in the courtship process. You simply wait patiently until "the power" will, at the proper time, present this one person to you. When this happens you will know it, and you should marry that person. It is assumed that to marry this person will guarantee you marriage happiness and that you could never have marriage happiness with anyone else.

I personally reject this "one and only" idea as false. It is pure gobbledygook. I can understand why many fine young people in our day believe in it. The adults of my generation have taught it to them. It is a deduction from the Hollywood false romance idea that boy meets girl, they fall in love at first sight, and the new lover is the "one and only." Thus, they must get married at once. But this whole idea is out of line with reality.

It is also a deduction from the theological idea of *extreme* predestination, the belief that God alone selects your marriage companion. You are completely passive in the process. This, too, is out of line with theological reality. Middle-of-the-road theology assumes both (1) the sovereignty of God (He is all-powerful) and (2) the freedom of man. Man respects the sovereignty of God and God respects the freedom of man. Although these two ideas seem to be contradictory, they are both real and work together beautifully in life's realities.

Why don't we be realistic and admit that space, time, and individual circumstances are major influences as we select marriage partners? Why did not John Jones, age twenty-one, who married Jane Doe, age twenty, last month in Atlanta, marry Ruby Smith? John Jones lived in Atlanta; Ruby Smith, in California. *Space!* When Ruby Smith was ready to marry, John Jones was not yet born. This presents a problem. *Time!* Ruby Smith was a Republican, while southern John Jones was a Democrat. *Circumstances!*

To be realistic, I would like to defend the theory that either John Jones or Jane Doe could court, learn to love, marry, and have a happy marriage with any one of several possibilities. Let me illustrate. After John Jones graduated from the local junior college, his parents agreed that he could go to any Methodist college. He was free to choose. John spent three months trying to decide whether to enroll at a Texas college or a Tennessee college. He could have chosen either one. Finally, he chose the Texas college. His roommate, a junior, was a member of the college social group. John went along with his roommate to a group meeting and met Jane Doe. They were attracted to each other. Across the weeks and months they dated, and after two years, they married. At this point, I am willing to say that they are each other's "one and only."

But, let us go back and suppose that John had selected the Tennessee college. He could have. There he would have had another roommate, attended another social occasion, and met another beautiful girl, Mary Johnson. They could have been attracted to each other, courted, married, and had a happy marriage. Then they would have been each other's "one and only." There are many different Methodist colleges John could have selected, and at each one were many fine prospects for marriage. Why don't we admit that space, time, and circumstances are major influences in selecting a marriage partner, and that we are free and active in the process?

The Bible teaches that our wonderful Creator-God, with infinite knowledge, can look forward in "foreknowledge" and know in advance which college John Jones will select and which girl he will choose in marriage (cf. Matthew 25:34; Romans 8:29; Ephesians 1:4; 1 Peter 1:20). But this infinite knowledge does not make John Jones a passive robot. He is free to choose. He actively participates in the choice.

In courtship and marriage, as in all of life, the sovereignty of God and the freedom of man work together beautifully. This leaves every John Jones and every Jane Doe *free* and *active,* and therefore *responsible,* in the processes of courtship and marriage.

SUPPOSE TWO PEOPLE WANT TO COURT YOU AND MARRY YOU. HOW DO YOU DECIDE BETWEEN THEM?

Cindy had been dating Tom for about a year, and they were going steady. He was nineteen; she was eighteen. They went to the same college and shared many of the college activities together. They both seemed very happy until Cindy met John. She had several classes with John, and they were attracted to each other. John knew Cindy was going steady with Tom. As the weeks went by, Cindy and John gradually became very close friends. One day John asked her for a date. At first, it was easy to refuse him because of Tom, but as the weeks went by, it became harder and harder for her to say no. She found that she really wanted to date John, but she could not because she was going steady with Tom. She became more miserable as the days went by. She no longer felt comfortable with either Tom or John. She didn't want to hurt either of them, yet she knew she must make a decision, both for their sake and for her sake. How should Cindy solve her problem?

When a girl has two fine boys interested in her, with marriage in mind, she is at the fork of the road! If she were just fourteen years old, her problem would be rather small. But if she is twenty-one, the normal age for girls to be serious about marriage, she has a major problem. She can string along with two people for one or two months without harm, provided they both know about it. But when this continues for more than two months, it is time for her to decide between the two. How should she make the decision? I suggest that she order a court-ship analysis test from The American Institute of Family Relations, 5287 Sunset Boulevard, Los Angeles, California, 90027. She should study the test carefully with the two suitors in mind and, in privacy, write out in detail the advantages and disadvantages of each. She must be honest about the facts. Using a test like this will help her think through her problem more thoroughly than she can with-out it.

Also, it would be well for her to confide in and seek counsel from some close friend who can stand off and look at her problem a little more objectively than she can. She should be sure to discuss her dilemma with her par-ents, but should not let them make this decision. This is her decision. Of course, she should make her problem a serious matter of prayer. A conference with her pastor or other Christian counselor is in order.

She will want to evaluate such things as companionship, communication, morals, Christian values and beliefs, age, family background, emotional maturity, future ambitions, occupation, integrity, and many other things.

She could study and weigh the facts about both suitors, plus the facts concerning herself and her personality. She should be sure to consider her inner feelings. They are important. But so are dozens of external facts. After thor-ough study she must make a decision. It should be an intelligent, rational decision. She should set an early date, say in two weeks, and make the decision! From that time on, she should continue dating one, and cease dating the other. Now, she should turn her feelings and emotions loose, and act on the intelligent decision she has made. She should not stop and ponder the decision, wondering if she made a mistake. She should move on, taking posi-tive action based on her decision. Love grows in intensity and maturity with the amount of positive effort one puts into it. Ultimate and complete love will not "drop on" anyone, like a chunk of plaster falling from the ceiling.

Note the procedure I have suggested: Feelings and emotions must be guided by intelligence, rationality, and the reality of facts. But do not leave feelings and emotions out of this decision.

Since we are finite, limited creatures, it is possible for anyone to follow the above procedure and still make the wrong decision. Six months later, one might have to break off with the person of his choice, as cold experience convinces him it will not work. It is necessary to warn that the chances of turning back to the rejected suitor are very, very slim. Such efforts have succeeded, but the rule is that his hurt ego and his loss of status will block any further relationships.

One last word, *do not* continue dating and holding on to both boys (or girls) indefinitely! Do not continue to become emotionally involved with the two people! If you do, in the end someone is going to get hurt! One of them may be *you!* So, make a decision, and move on. Keep on making right decisions directed by intelligent, mature values and following divine leadership. Follow this path and you will find that life is challenging and good, and filled with fertile, fruitful meaning.

SHOULD I MARRY "BEAUTIFUL BETTY" OR "BALANCED BETTY"?

All people enjoy the beautiful—a rainbow, a sunset, a violin solo, an honest life, or a beautiful young woman. This is good. It is a part of human nature. Yet in the realm of courtship and marriage an overemphasis on the "beautiful woman" can be dangerous. The propaganda media, including Hollywood movies and slick color magazines, tend to exaggerate the importance of female beauty. Young men, because of their intense sex drive, tend to seek in courtship and marriage the girl who is physically beautiful, or, stated in another way, they seek the young girl who appeals to them sexually. This is not an unworthy consideration; however, it must not be the first (it is sometimes the only) concern in selecting a marriage partner!

Often the young man chases "Beautiful Betty" in courtship. The competition is keen and fierce. A dozen or two other males are after her. At long last, after continued determination and persistence, he wins the physical beauty queen, and they make a final social splash with a $5,000 wedding. Do they live happily ever after? Maybe! Sometimes! But too often, six months later, the young husband wakes up from his unrealistic dream to realize that instead of having a happy marriage, he has been caught in a deadly trap. He is married to a selfish, lazy, discontented nag.

Why? Beauty can be vain (Proverbs 31:30). Physical beauty alone is phony, counterfeit. Too many compliments can be harmful. Ever since "Beautiful Betty" was a little child, hundreds of people had given her flattering compliments until she became proud and self-centered. Her only ambition was to appear to others as the perfect beauty queen. Her parents promoted this. Thus for twenty years "Beautiful Betty" has basked in the halo of her physical beauty and failed to develop the other personality qualities necessary to happiness in life and in marriage. It is not difficult to imagine the future of such a marriage.

Unfortunately, the boys who chase "Beautiful Betty" tend to bypass and reject, as courtship prospects, many girls who might not enter a Hollywood beauty contest but who have developed well-balanced personality traits. These girls have such traits as plans for the future, concern for others, unselfishness, humility, sympathy, modesty, frugality, and balanced spiritual, mental, moral, and social graces and values. These are the building blocks that form a stable foundation for a happy life and marriage. They are far more precious than jewels. When a boy, through the courtship processes, associates with "Balanced Betty" and learns the nature of her inner personality, he learns to appreciate and love her. Her physical appearance, which he had at first rejected as average, now becomes the most attractive, the most beautiful he knows. We all can probably recall one or more such experiences in which, on first meeting certain persons, we were not impressed with them. But when we later associated with them as friends, becoming acquainted with the total person, we found them to be true-blue, balanced individuals.

But this discussion of "Beautiful Betty" must not be misunderstood. We must not discriminate against "beauty" as such. Our Creator must have loved beauty, since He created so much of it. Could we say that everything God has created is good and beautiful, including you and me? It is only human misuse of beautiful things that becomes ugly. We must not discriminate against "beautiful" girls. If a girl is physically beautiful, this ought to cause her to be thankful and humble, and to use her beauty in an unselfish life. A young man who is blessed with a sweetheart who has balanced inner personality traits plus external physical beauty is fortunate. Both before and after marriage, he should strive to allow these qualities to bring out the best in both of them in a life of Christian service. This will bring happiness. It will preserve and develop their fine qualities to become even finer through the years.

Compliments, charm, and grace can be deceptive. Physical beauty can be vain because it is not lasting; but the woman who has strength of character, who is steadfast in goodness, and who follows the inner, intelligent, Spirit-led guidelines of the Creator shall be praised.

IS "DUTCH DATING" SOCIALLY ACCEPTABLE?

In the early rural days in our society girls seldom worked for pay and had access to little or no money. We followed the patriarchal tradition of the boy asking and paying for the date. During the past fifty years the job and economic market has opened up to girls, and many social traditions have been modified. As a rule, boys probably still have access to more money than girls. But since girls now have access to some money, they are asking, "Why can't we volunteer to share half of the dating expense on certain occasions in order to be sure of a date with that certain boy?"

In my opinion, dutch dating (or dutch treating) is a good and acceptable practice within certain reasonable guidelines. In fact, I recommend it for mature young people within the normal courtship age. When two mature young people of normal courtship age like each other and want to date each other, it is not important which one pays for the date. The fact that the boy may be working his way through college and is short on money should not block the couple's courtship. For her to share part (or even all) of the expenses on some dates is just good common sense. In fact, it is practiced far more than most of us realize.

Since society still assumes that the boy should pay for the date, girls should follow certain rules, carefully, when dutch dating. *Rule 1:* The girl must bring the matter up, offering to share in the expense. *Rule 2:* The girl must keep the fact of the dutch date a secret. *Rule 3:* When the date involves the purchase of tickets, the girl must secretly give her boyfriend the money to purchase the tickets. When they approach the ticket booth to purchase tickets to the concert or the basketball game, a responsible young man is not about to allow couples following them to see her buy her own ticket, or both hers and his. In our culture this would be ego-defeating to the boy. *Rule 4:* Do not use the practice of dutch dating too often. *Rule 5:* Always remember the young man's pride. Avoid undermining his ego. He is not a lazy no-good. Often he is working in circumstances over which he has no control. Help him to maintain his self-esteem.

Unfortunately, the drift of courtship expense in our society is continually upward, being escalated by the greed of vested interests and excess social sophistication. Often the expense of an average date may be ten dollars. On special occasions twenty-five to fifty dollars may be demanded. It is unfortunate, indeed, that the wonderful process of courtship should be blocked by such expensive social excesses. Allow me to repeat here that when two fine young people both like each other and want to date, they should not allow such a minor thing as who pays how much of the necessary expense to block their courtship. For a young man to cooperate in the above-described circumstances is not a reflection on his character.

At this point I would like to scold and warn the girl who is not interested in a date unless it involves spending much money. A boy will not be interested in her very long. He will soon recognize her as the real "gold-digger" that she is and will quickly drop her like a "wet sock." This bit of advice needs to be reversed. I would like to scold and warn the boy who has access to plenty of money but refuses to go on any kind of date that involves spending a little money. A girl will not be interested in such a boy very long. She will soon recognize him for the "miser" and "skinflint" that he really is and will quickly drop him like a "wet dish rag."

It is not necessary to spend a large sum of money on formal folderol in order to have a good date. Just being together, enjoying pleasant fellowship, and, through little initiatives and responses developing and crystallizing a little farther, a genuine interest in each other is real courtship progress. Often those dates where the most money is spent may turn out to be the least profitable.

WOUNDED IN COURTSHIP: AN EXAMPLE

By making wrong decisions in courtship, young people can easily bring major problems on themselves. The following letter from Carol and my personal reply to her is illustrative.

> **I am seventeen years old and dating a man thirty-eight. I always thought sex was supposed to be wonderful, but my Sunday school teacher told me that it was not, unless you were married, because it is against the commandments of God. I didn't believe her then, but I do now. You see**

I have been having sex with this man for three years. We dated three months without sex. I was a virgin and did not agree with his ideas about sex. He kept saying that if I would have sex with him it would make him love me more. I believed him and gave in. Now, I wish I had never met him. We were supposed to be married over two years ago. He has not mentioned it for over a year. I love to be around people and go to parties, but all he wants to do on our dates is park in one of several secret places he has picked out, or go to the drive-in movie. He has no interest in the movie. What it all boils down to is that we have sex and then he is ready to go home. He makes excuses that he has to get up early the next morning and work. He takes me home, kisses me two or three times and walks me to the door and that's it. These dates are extremely boring to me. Sometimes I get so nervous just thinking what a fool I have been that I wind up smoking two or three packs of cigarettes a day. A couple of times I have gotten drunk, because it helps me to forget everything. Sometimes I think I love him enough to wait until he is ready to marry me. Do you think that if we ever did get married that it would be a happy marriage? Please warn other young girls not to make a fool of themselves as I have. Will you give me some advice? How can I get out of this situation and build a happy life?

Carol

Carol, your marriage to this man will never take place. It is obvious, even to you, from your letter, that his only interest in you is sexual gratification. He does not love you. Love does not exploit the person loved. He is old enough to be your father. When you were born, he was twenty-one years old. Men in the United States live to an average age of sixty-seven and women to be seventy-four. Assuming his death at sixty-seven, you would be forty-six. Thus you would be a widow for approximately twenty-eight years. If you did marry him, your marriage would probably end in a rather quick divorce. If you are so unhappy with him now, what would the situation be after marriage? Multiply by about three.

Even though you say you love him, your letter indicates that you do not. You are bored with his dates. You know he is not honest with you. He has broken his marriage promise. He tricked you to violate your ideals that sex belongs to marriage by the old, male double-cross, namely, "If you submit to me, it will make me love you more." Your letter indicates that this man began to violate you at the tender age of fourteen. (I am wondering why your parents allowed you at fourteen to date a man thirty-five.) These relationships have made you into a nervous wreck. Two or three packs a day and drunkenness against your will! Now really, do you love him? No! You hate him!

You ask for advice about the future. You must sever all relationship with him at once. Don't be disappointed when the break does not bother him. When you refuse him, he will drop you and move on to the next victim.

Now as to your future, Carol, you have many things going for you. You are very young. I assume you are in high school and in good physical health. Be sure to finish high school and get as much education as possible. You are now closer to your Sunday school teacher and church than before, as sad experience has proven their ideals to be right. You are stronger and more mature now in that you will think twice before walking into other traps. Your present "nerves-on-edge" feeling is due to disappointment and guilt feelings. You have been gravely wounded emotionally and spiritually by one you thought you loved. Have you noticed that when you sober up after getting drunk, that your problem is still there? The only thing I know that can calm your nerves and wipe out your past is to ask God to forgive you for violating what your Sunday school teacher called "the commandments of God," and commit your life to Christ as your personal Savior (John 1:12; 5:24; 14:6). There is no other alternative. The Bible tells us that when we ask God for forgiveness, His forgiveness is complete. He literally makes the wounded whole. In His sight the wound is healed and you are as if it had never happened. Accept this forgiveness. (Read Isaiah 1:18; Psalm 103:12; Jeremiah 31:34; Micah 7:19; John 8:11.)

You must also forgive yourself. Do not allow this experience to cause you to hate and reject love, courtship, men, marriage, sex, and parenthood. As you continue in school, develop your self-confidence. Smile. Hold your head high. Move out of your isolated life, back into the mainstream of social life. Make friends with mature young people. There are millions of them. You'll find them at school, at church, and at tennis courts and other athletic games. Continue the processes of courtship, selecting the boy of your choice, with your age and interests. You are worthy of his love. At the proper age and time move into marriage. You are worthy of and deserve a good marriage and a happy family life.

4

Going Steady

WHAT IS THE RELATION OF GOING STEADY TO AGE?

Young people generally enter high school at the age of fourteen or fifteen and graduate at age seventeen or eighteen. They usually graduate from college at about age twenty-two. There is a major difference between the process of casual dating (dating the field) and going steady. Generally, in casual dating, the couple is not in love. They like each other but both are free to date others. Judson and Mary Landis distinguish between "casually dating" and "steadily dating." In steady dating, a boy and girl continue to date each other often, and seldom date anyone else, yet there is no special agreement and both are free to date others.[1] Both casual dating and steady dating are social relationships and fellowship for the purpose of developing competence and self-confidence in associating with the opposite sex. This type of dating is an effort not only to understand the opposite sex, but also to understand self in relation to the opposite sex. On the other hand, in going steady, the couple are usually older and more mature. They "think" they are in love with each other. They have a definite understanding that they will be faithful to each other. Neither is free to date anyone else.

Research indicates there are three major differences be-

[1] Judson T. Landis and Mary G. Landis, *Building a Successful Marriage*, 5th ed. (New York: Prentice-Hall, 1968), p. 43.

tween going steady and not going steady in high school and in college. (1) Going steady in high school represents dating security. Both boy and girl can be certain of a date at regular social occasions. Those who are not going steady may or may not draw a date. (2) Going steady represents social status. The influence of the peer group is strong. Those who are not going steady tend to envy those who are. (3) Going steady in high school often is not associated with possible marriage.

Going steady in college also involves a degree of dating security and social status, but it is more definitely associated with interest in marriage. It is a commitment to study the possibility of whether or not each loves the other and if each is a good marriage risk.

Somewhere in the process of courtship, teenagers should cease casual dating and move to the level of going steady. For a boy to "date the field" until he is age twenty-one to twenty-five indicates the existence of major emotional problems. For children to go steady before puberty (while still in childhood) indicates major emotional problems of their parents and may do irreparable damage to the children. There needs to be a middle ground.

It is impossible to set up a specific age where youth begin to go steady. Some are more mature at fifteen than others at twenty. Ages fifteen and sixteen are usually the casual dating periods. Some mature young people could safely go steady during the senior year of high school. Others should wait until college age. Most sociologists and parents object to high-school engagements. Probably most parents think going steady should wait until after high-school graduation.

It is a fact that in America young people have more courtship freedom than in any other nation. In many cultures there is little or no courtship before marriage. This has been true in India. Romance and courtship are seldom practiced in that country. Marriages are arranged by the parents. Often a boy and girl never see each other until marriage. Some parents allow them to see (not date) each other once before marriage. Some parents allow them to see only a photograph of each other. Girls of India do not object to this. To do so would be bold. In the large cities a few educated parents allow the boys to have veto power. Many parents use the horoscope (location of the stars) in their choice of a daughter's husband. This is pure superstition and "hocus-pocus."

In our society we have personalized courtship. Young people have much freedom in courtship practices and in selecting a husband or wife, and rightly so. But money interests, social climbers, and the propaganda media have promoted such unlimited courtship freedom and an overemphasis on sex that it has led to immorality, babies born out of wedlock, and divorces. We need a middle ground, including freedom, with some limitations.

For parents to force their children to date certain people indicates that the parents themselves have major emotional problems and a lack of understanding concerning the needs and rights of their children. For youth in their early teens to demand from their parents complete courtship freedom without any limitations indicates extreme immaturity on their part. Most teenagers need and welcome some mature adult guidance in their courtship practices.

Dating security and social status are not sufficient grounds for going steady. Going steady is an important and essential part of courtship. It is a serious trial period during which a couple makes an intelligent analysis as to whether they are a good marriage risk by thoroughly studying each other's emotional, moral, spiritual, social, and economic characteristics.

WHAT PERSONAL QUALITIES SHOULD YOUNG PEOPLE LOOK FOR IN SELECTING A MARRIAGE COMPANION?

No one person possesses all good qualities. Happy marriages are between two imperfect people who adjust to each other's imperfections. There is no perfect blueprint, nor is there a perfect building. Yet it would be foolish to try to build an important building without a blueprint. It is good for young people to have the best blueprint possible to check carefully the personal qualities of a possible marriage partner. Historical experience plus much sociological research has led us to a rather clear picture of the better qualities of marriage partners.

1. A prospective marriage partner should believe in God the infinite Creator back of the universe and life and accept the permanent truths and principles inherent in both the Creator and the created, including the Ten Commandments. Courtship and marriage should flow from this tested, balanced, value system that modern youth call the "eternal triangle"—you, me, and God.

2. One's sweetheart should possess self-confidence, not in the sense of egotism or an offensive air of superiority, but rather with a positive feeling that he is going to meet and work through life's problems.

3. He should possess the quality of self-discipline and self-control. He should have reasonable control over his bodily appetites, his thoughts, his temper, and his relationships with all people.

4. He should have ambition and purpose, including positive short-range and long-range life's goals. He should have had experience in responsible work. He should show initiative, be thorough, punctual, and give close attention to details.

5. He should be willing to admit his own mistakes, take the responsibility for them, and profit by them. Dr. J. E. Dillard used to say, "When the same man is bitten by the same dog, under the same circumstances, the second time, it's time to shoot the man instead of the dog."

6. He should have mature ideas about how to handle money and things. He should not be a miser and worship them, neither should he be a prodigal spendthrift. There ought to be a middle ground. There is reason to suspect any twenty-year-old youth who does not have any kind of savings account and has never had one.

7. He should reflect a love, respect, and appreciation

for his home, his parents, and his brothers and sisters. He should possess love and appreciation for little children.

8. He should respect and appreciate the personal and individual rights, dignity, and freedom of all other people. He should try to look beyond their weaknesses to their strong qualities. In human relationships he should be gentle, patient, sympathetic (feeling for), and empathetic (feeling with). He should listen to the points of view of other people, yet he should be an individual and do independent thinking.

9. He should have a sense of humor, including the ability to laugh at himself. In courtship and marriage shared laughter builds strong ties.

10. He should have a balanced sex education and philosophy. He should be neither ascetic (the flesh and sex are evil) nor hedonistic (pleasure is the primary purpose of life). There ought to be a middle ground.

11. Prospective marriage partners should appeal to each other physically. This is right and normal. External physical appeal often changes when we get acquainted with the person's inner attitudes and values. Certainly physical appeal is not an unworthy concern in selecting a marriage partner.

12. A prospective marriage partner ought to have the quality of contentment and happiness. Happy people are healthy people. They are the people who love and serve and succeed. In *Les Miserables* Victor Hugo had Jean Valjean say, "It is nothing to die. It is an awful thing never to have lived!"

Any young person looking for these qualities in a marriage companion should work diligently to develop these qualities in himself or herself.

WHAT QUALITIES SHOULD YOUNG PEOPLE AVOID IN SELECTING A MARRIAGE COMPANION?

Just as the health department warns against the enemies of good health, so young people need to be warned against

certain attitudes, activities, and patterns of behavior that
are the enemies of a healthy marriage.

1. A girl (or boy) should avoid a prospective marriage
partner whose regular dress and grooming are untidy, care-
less, and sloppy. Persons are not responsible for such traits
as tallness or shortness, but they are responsible for cleanliness, neatness, and personal appearance. Cleanliness is
next to godliness.

2. Young people should avoid courtship with an extreme
introvert, that is, one who withdraws from social interaction and spends much time isolated as a hermit inside his
private mental castle. When in contact with society such
a person may tend to be easily offended, to demand sympathy, and to have moods of depression. He may feel
inferior, insecure, and undersell himself both to himself
and to others.

3. Young people should avoid courtship with those who
seemingly cannot make independent and wise decisions.
Such prospects may be dependent on parents, friends, or
sweetheart for all decisions. In courtship they are looking
for an "authority figure" instead of a sweetheart and a
marriage companion.

4. Young people should avoid courtship with persons
who are self-centered, conceited, and possess a dictatorial
and domineering attitude. These tend to look with arro-
gance and disdain on lowly people. They often overestimate their importance and pose as supersophisticated
snobs. They may be first-class bullies instead of being can-
didates for courtship. They are fit subjects for pity and
prayer.

5. Young people should avoid courtship with those
who have little or no self-control. The behavior of those
who lack self-control is usually determined by feelings and
emotions, not by facts, reason, intelligence, or "holy writ."
They have to have their own way about everything. They
want what they want when they want it. They have no
capacity for adjustment or compromise. They enjoy hurting people, seeking revenge. They are lazy and dependent

financially. They violate the opposite sex at will. They are often characterized by two packs a day, a pint a week, and vulgar language.

6. Young people should avoid courtship with persons with no socially accepted moral standards or values. They are often cynics (those who sneer at what is right and good) and iconoclasts (those who tear down and destroy all religious beliefs). They rebel against the churches, the Bible, and the Ten Commandments. They often pose as scientists and taunt Christian young people by saying, "Where is your scientific proof that there is a God?" The fact that they have never had any Christian experience with God in Christ, or that they have no scientific proof that there is no God, does not seem to bother their self-appointed "Pontifical Excellencies."

7. Young people should avoid courtship with those persons whom psychologists, sociologists, and counselors call "sociopathic personalities." They are aptly described by four Lutheran scholars in the excellent book *What Then Is Man?* Sociopathic persons

> are unable to adjust to society on what might be termed a "moral" level. They have no evidence of possessing a conscience or of being able to develop one. In fact they seem markedly free of anxiety.... He shows no guilt ... he seems satisfied with his way of living.... These people have an inability to delay their gratifications and work toward distant goals....They react poorly to routine, resent discipline and authority, and like to "stir up some excitement." In spite of their superficial sociability, they are basically cold, unable to form deep emotional relationships to others, and they ... exploit those about them. These people may be highly intelligent, with a misleading charm which leads people into believing their stories.[2]

8. Finally, young people should avoid courtship with persons who thinks of sex as an end in itself. They often think that sex is all there is to life and have little or no interest in anything else. This attitude is true of the boys

[2] Graduate Study Number III, *What Then Is Man?* (St. Louis: Concordia Publishing House, 1958), pp. 137, 138.

who insist that a girl prove her love to them. When a boy becomes aggressive with a girl on the first date and says, "I love you," what he really means is "I need you."

All young people who avoid those who possess these qualities in selecting a marriage companion should work diligently to avoid these qualities in their own lives.

WHAT ARE APPROPRIATE GIFTS TO GIVE DURING THE GOING-STEADY PERIOD?

When a boy and girl love each other, or think they love each other, or would like to develop love for each other, the matter of giving gifts is important. It is a must!

When deciding what gifts to give during courtship, consider asking the following questions: (1) At what stage is your courtship—casual dating, going steady, or engagement? (2) Why do you want to give a gift? (3) How much money should you spend? (4) What will fit the receiver's personality, Christian values, and needs? (5) What will the receiver not hesitate to accept? (6) What will the receiver's parents and friends think about the gift?

It is rather difficult to draw a line between casual dating, going steady, and engagement. Yet these three levels of courtship are meaningful in discussing the procedures and problems involved. Therefore we will relate appropriate gifts for the going-steady period with those given during casual dating and engagement.

In the beginning of casual dating, a gift indicates that one is not only happy with the new relationship but also interested in continuing it. In casual dating, a gift should be meaningful yet not too personal. It should be inexpensive. A gift that is too expensive seems to say, "I'll buy your love with this present" or "I've given you something expensive, now you owe me something expensive in return." A gift that is too personal, such as underclothing, indicates very poor taste. It causes embarrassment, parental objection, and implies a too-intimate relationship. In the beginning of casual dating the first gift should probably be a carefully selected greeting card appropriate for the occasion that expresses a compliment and indicates a further personal interest. Other suggested gifts could be a record, candy, inexpensive jewelry, books, key chains, homemade cookies, minor car accessories, or stationery. A boy should be careful about giving a girl flowers during casual dating. They seem to say, "I'm really falling in love with you." She may read much more into them than he meant.

When a mature couple is going steady, it is acceptable to give more expensive and personal gifts. Gifts suitable during casual dating are still acceptable. To that list can be added flowers, Bibles, rings, outer clothing (such as sweaters, jackets, ties, scarfs, gloves, and belts), pocketbooks, wallets, cosmetics, perfume, cologne, pictures, engraved jewelry, a musical jewelry box, poetry, long-distance calls, and tapes.

During engagement all of these gifts are in order. Other gifts would include things both can use in the future such as towels, shaving kits, radios, record players, tape recorders, television sets, and minor household items.

There are several general principles one should follow in giving gifts. At any period during courtship a boy should be careful about giving candy if his sweetheart is a "weight watcher." She might be embarrassed. Gifts given during the going-steady period should be meaningful at the time and yet easy to live with should the couple break up. Monographed gifts for girls during engagement are not recommended since it is assumed that her initials will soon be changed. The giver during engagements should consider the fact that from one-third to one-half of all engagements are broken. The giver should consider whether the engagement is "skating on thin ice" or whether it is on solid ground and certain to culminate in a good marriage. Some engaged couples agree on inexpensive gifts in order to save money for the expenses of the wedding and honeymoon. It is meaningful for sweethearts to give each other surprise gifts for no special reason except to show love and appreciation.

Courtship and love go together. Love and giving go together. Tactful, thoughtful giving at the right time promotes and develops love on the part of both the giver and the receiver. We may give without loving, but we cannot love without giving!

WHEN YOUR SWEETHEART DRIFTS FROM YOU—AN EXAMPLE.

Sometimes during the going-steady period one of the couple begins to drift away from his first love. Dates grow farther apart and when the two people are together, their relationships tend to be formal, routine, shallow, and often boring. The former enthusiasm, warmth, and interpersonal glow and understandings are gone. Such was the case with Joe and Martha. They had dated for over a year. They had gone steady for nine months and had a secret preengagement understanding. Martha wrote, "We love each other very much." Joe was placed on a night shift at his work and did not come to see Martha very often. He had always liked to associate with a group of boys who were close friends. Martha wrote that "he spends his spare time with the boys on weekends. He thinks he should have the freedom to go as he pleases with the boys and not come to see me. How do I let him know that he has a responsibility to come to see me when he has time to come? What can I say to him about his friends without hurting him?"

After Martha's description of Joe's behavior, I am wondering about her statement, "We both love each other very much." Now really, do they? Martha loves him, yes, but does he love her? Honest now! Maybe he did some months ago, but does he now? Something seems to have cooled his love. You see, one in love does not act the way Joe is acting. If he loved Martha "very much," he would be seeing her every weekend and at every other time possible. He would be calling her often and maybe writing her some letters. Love operates like this. I understand why Martha loves Joe, but I think she should admit to herself that she is living in a world of fantasy and make-believe. She is calling black, white. She ought to respond to the reality that she is now "second fiddle." Joe thinks more of the boys than he does of her. Marriage under these circumstances could turn sour. It could be disaster.

Now, what can Martha and other fine young people do to win their sweethearts back? This is the burden of Martha's heart and her letter. I answered Martha in the following manner. I suggested, negatively, that she should not try to force her drifting sweetheart. She should not be possessive and should avoid excessive jealousy. She should not nag nor appear spineless. She should not use sex as a method and weapon to force her sweetheart to love her. This would "boomerang." She should not allow this trying experience to destroy her self-confidence. Even if she should lose Joe, she should not allow this to frighten her away from the opposite sex, courtship, love, and marriage. She should not become bitter and pessimistic.

Positively, she should face frankly what seems to be the real reasons why Joe is neglecting her. She should list the possibilities and study them carefully. She should examine her attitudes, characteristics, and behavior for possible problems, and attempt to improve any weak areas in her own life. She should be neat and attractive, smile, and use compliments. She should reexamine her lover's attitudes and characteristics and compare them with her standards for life and for marriage. She should seek counsel from a close personal friend, pastor, or some other qualified counselor.

If she feels that there is a strong possibility that she could win her sweetheart back, she will eventually have to have a showdown, that is, bring the problem out into the open and discuss it thoroughly. She should arrange for a "conference" where there is privacy and plenty of time for the two to talk. At the conference she should not appear angry, but be kind, thoughtful, and self-confident. She should explain positively how she feels. She should express her continued love and interest in her future marriage. But she should explain that reason insists that she cannot continue as "second fiddle." She should say, "I do not want to break up with you, but I cannot afford to continue in such a one-sided emotional involvement." She should hope for an apology and a renewal of concern; yet she should be prepared for a rejection. She should give time for an answer if it is requested. Unless she receives some genuine, positive response and assurance in words and attitudes from her sweetheart, within a reasonable length of time, she has no other choice but to break off her "one-way street" relationship and turn her courtship interest and attention toward others. Even if she loves, she should come out of this experience a stronger, wiser person. Thousands of others have done so.

5

Your Parents and Your Courtship

HOW SHOULD TEENAGERS HANDLE
PARENT-CHILD CONFLICT?

Attention, teenager! So you've finally reached that "golden age" (the teen years), but these days of "puppy love," going steady, rings, broken hearts, and parent-itis are not all they are cracked up to be. Right? This is especially true when those parents of yours are always nagging, prying, snooping, and bossing. That's the way you see it now, isn't it? Okay. So let's look at this case of parent-itis for a while; and let's look at the situation calmly, objectively, and maturely.

Let's imagine you are the parent and your parent is you (too difficult?). Next, attribute your attitudes and behavior to them and begin analyzing. How would you react to your own mannerisms and behavior if you were in their shoes? Now let's discuss other ways of bridging the gap between you and them.

How many times a day do you violate your parents' trust in you? Lying about destinations and other facets of dating is underhanded, immature, and inconsiderate. Sneaking out, whether to off-limit places or seeing a person secretly, "goes against the grain." Anything that may violate your parents' code of ethics (smoking, drinking, using drugs, profanity, immorality) will naturally put a barrier between you and them. Is this what you really want? Just who is the real problem, you or your parents?

Do you ever misuse the freedom your parents have given you? Parents set rules and regulations out of a life's experience and for a purpose—to help you grow up! Violating the freedoms and restrictions set up by these rules can also be seen as signs of selfishness (along with immaturity) and a lack of a sense of responsibility. These may also be described as a "gimme attitude." Many times you make unreasonable requests of your parents and think you should be allowed to do anything, go anywhere, and have everything—with no strings attached. Again, is this what you really want? Being self-centered, selfish, and inconsiderate of family members will not exactly make you a glorious child in their eyes! There are times when you must take "time-out" from yourself and check the needs, wants, and ideas of your parents.

Sometimes you think that your parents think they know it all and that you know more than your parents. Now really, do you? You may consider that your parents' moral code is out-of-date and unfair and certainly doesn't apply to your day and age. Let me let you in on a little secret. Times do change, but good, basic moral codes and beliefs do not change! Don't question your parents' values. They are intelligent human beings, too! You must not be impulsive in thinking there is no tomorrow, that you must have everything now; one day you may just carry this too far. Remember, you don't have all the answers, just as your parents don't, and you can't very well get along without their care and advice. How about giving some credit where credit is due—to your parents?

Do you criticize your parents? Many teenagers do. And then do you still expect your parents to hand over everything you want when you want it? Do you also expect them to be there when you need them? You may even expect them to overlook all of your mistakes! Criticism, on your part, usually makes you look worse than the parents you're criticizing. This type of behavior embarrasses your parents and distorts both your social image and theirs. Think before you talk!

Many times during your courtship period your parents may feel slightly unwanted or unneeded; you should be sensitive to these feelings. Your pulling away from the nest is expected; but it is alarming and frightening when it actually happens. Try to understand their problem, and let them have a chance to understand yours. Your parents are interested in and concerned for you. They love you. Don't rob them of knowing your dates or of the seriousness of your courtship. I know yours is an age of mobility where you really need to be somewhere all the time, but parents need and want a few minutes of your time to talk to you and your date.

Finally, I would like to consider stubbornness! Once again, you have that "know-it-all" attitude and refuse to listen to anything. Naturally, you regard the approval and advice of your peers as being superior to that of your parents. You're out to prove your parents wrong because you resent their authority over you. You usually approach this in many ways: (1) You simply won't understand the word "no." (2) You're not willing to cooperate or communicate. (3) You promptly give the silent treatment! Exactly where is this getting you? Is this not ugly stubbornness?

Okay. Stop! Think! You should realize that all these ideas discussed above are real problem areas and that you may have been guilty of some or all of these at least some particular time in your life. Now, go say a few kind words to your parents; they love you and need some love from you. And, as you can see, they've had some rough days!

WHY DO PARENTS WORRY ABOUT THEIR CHILDREN'S COURTSHIP?

During the early courtship years, most young people have some conflict with their parents over rules and regulations about their dating. Sometimes the conflict is mild, and at other times it is extreme, involving emotional scenes. The following letter is an example of mild conflict.

I am in college, am nineteen years old, and am an only

child. I live in a dormitory. Letters, telephone calls, and visits from my parents are frequent. I enjoy this contact with them, but it is clear that they are greatly WORRIED about my courtship. I make good grades. I have never been in jail. I have never been arrested. I love and appreciate my parents. They are paying my way through college. I am getting along well. Yet, it bothers me that they worry about me and my dating. They started to worry about me when I was in high school and began going out on dates. My question is, why do my parents worry about my courtship?
Jim

Jim has asked a question that thousands of other fine young people wonder about. I would like to change his word "worry" to the word "concern." The average teenager's parents *are concerned* about them for many reasons. Parents *love* their children dearly. Why? They are "bone of their bone and flesh of their flesh."

Now let us trace the life experience of an average teenager with his or her parents which will reveal other significant reasons for parental concern. The nine-month period from conception until birth was a period of sacrifice in which a mother experienced morning sickness and pre-birth movement (some babies kick like a mule—well, almost), made many trips to the doctor, tolerated enlarged body shape, and endured anxiety over the baby's possible health at birth.

At birth, in spite of the efficiency of modern doctors, a mother travels through an uncertain period. During pregnancy and birth, a father is as sympathetic and understanding of his wife as he knows how to be. He wants to help, but often feels helpless.

When parents take their new baby from the hospital, they write checks totalling $600 or more to cover hospital room, delivery room, anesthetic, doctor's fee, tests, medicine, and other essentials.

During the first few years of life a baby is helpless. Parents constantly have to shadow, shield, protect, feed, and train him. When the baby is about twelve to fifteen months old and starts walking, parents have to "child-proof" the home to protect the baby from himself as he begins to explore the world about him. Dr. James Dobson calls a child at this age a "toddler," and aptly says, "A toddler has a tiger in his tank."

From the day of birth until age 19, parents have to spend much time every day and every week to protect, guide, and lead their child through those years. Using their best judgment, their only concern is to bring their child to adult maturity as a well-balanced, total person.

Suppose Jim's parents had decided not to have any children and instead had spent all of their time and money in getting an advanced education for themselves. They would both now have an M.A. and possibly a Ph.D. degree in their chosen fields. Or suppose they had spent this time and money on studying violin; if they had talent, they would probably both now be concert violinists. But they wanted Jim. They loved him. They were partners with God in his creation.

Speaking of money, parents have spent between $20,000 and $30,000 to bring a child to age nineteen. A college education may cost them approximately $10,000 more.

In the courtship period, young people will soon be choosing a marriage partner. This is a happy, yet crucial period in life. Evelyn Millis Duvall probably expresses the secret concern of parents for their children when she says,

> A major concern of parents is that their sons and daughters don't get caught in some sexual jam that will spoil their future for years to come . . . perhaps catapulting them into a ruined reputation, or a loveless, unhappy marriage. . . . They don't want to see their children hurt by situations or forces whose strength and urgency the young people may not be prepared to handle well.[1]

Also, parents are aware of evil men who write shallow love lyrics and pulp magazines that mislead young people into thinking that going steady, premarriage promiscuity, and marrying young is the "in thing" to do. They are aware

[1] Evelyn Millis Duvall, *The Art of Dating* (New York: Association Press, 1968), p. 193.

of the fact that at least 350,000 babies were born out of wedlock last year in the United States. They are aware of the headlines calling attention to the results of alcohol, drugs, and automobile accidents.

Thus we must conclude that parents do not want to make their children's decisions or select their dates and marriage partners. Nor do they want to run their lives. They simply want them to grow up strong, well, and happy, and to be mature Christians. Now, honestly, do not parents have a right to be concerned about their children's courtship? To be otherwise, they would be abnormal, unnatural, and delinquent as parents.

SHOULD A YOUNG PERSON INSIST ON COURTSHIP AND MARRIAGE WHEN HIS PARENTS STRONGLY OBJECT?

When parents object to a certain courtship and marriage, when brothers and sisters object, when other relatives and friends object, when seemingly everybody objects, the answer has to be no. Is it possible for the whole community to be wrong and two lovers right? I doubt it.

Sometimes parents use very poor psychology in objecting to their children's courtship and marriage. Instead of communicating and reasoning with their child, they firmly say a loud NO and throw up a stone wall of silence. Without realizing it, parents, who act this way are working against their own interests. Their inflexible objection drives a wedge between them and their daughter or son. When the flow of security from parents is cut off, to whom does he or she turn for security? To his or her sweetheart. Thus the poor psychology of the parents drives the young couple closer together.

On the other hand, young people often use much worse psychology than do parents in that they throw up a wall of silence by secretly planning marriage. Dr. Wayne Oates once told of a college freshman girl who, four months after she enrolled in college, called her mother, long distance, reversed the charges, and said, "Mother, Jim and

I are engaged and want to be married and want your approval." This was the first the mother had heard of Jim and the romance. The mother began to cry. When the girl's father got on the telephone and found what it was all about, he exploded and bawled out his daughter, saying no in objectionable language. Now, why did the parents object? Probably because they felt they had been rejected by their own daughter, who meant so much to them. The cause of young people's conflict with their parents on courtship matters is a two-way street.

When Mary's parents object to her courtship, I suggest that Mary ask her parents for a conference during which she will calmly ask them to list one, two, three, etc., the reasons why they object to her marriage. She may disarm them, if their only reason is that "we just can't consider giving up our darling little twelve-year-old daughter" (who is twenty). You see, a few insecure parents fail to move along with the clock of time and do not realize that their daughter is no longer a child but an adult who, as is normal, wants marriage. On the other hand, if in the conference, Mary's parents list the reasons for their objection, such as: (1) Your suitor has a long police record; (2) he has never worked a day in his life; (3) he has no plans for an occupation; (4) he has little or no respect for other people; (5) he is a religious cynic; (6) his moral values are nil; and (7) he is addicted to alcohol, then Mary's parents have disarmed her, if she is a mature, rational person. You see, in marriage, one has to live in society. You must plan a marriage that is acceptable to society, one that is rational, social, moral, and spiritual, and one that can survive. Furthermore, for Mary to marry against her parents' will is to set up a nearly impossible in-law situation that can only bring heartache and misery later.

Yes, under normal circumstances, I think young people twenty-one to twenty-two should be free to choose their own marriage companions. Their parents made their own decision, and youth should make theirs. But the choice should reflect intelligent, long-range, future planning. It should include scientific and moral facts about happiness in marriage. It must finally be based on divine leadership. It must not result from spur-of-the-moment emotions and sex. Your choice should consider the advice of your parents, relatives, friends, and pastor; but in the end, the choice must be yours.

Now, I want to be fair. There are isolated, exceptional, cases when I would recommend that mature young people, marry against the will of immature, insecure parents. I have made this recommendation more than once. For a person to stay imprisoned to such parents until he is forty or fifty years old is sad indeed. Yet, to marry against your parents' will should be the last resort of faithful love, and it should be done only after you have carefully prayed about it.

HOW CAN YOUNG PEOPLE DEVELOP A HEALTHY INDEPENDENCE FROM PARENTS AND AT THE SAME TIME DEVELOP A HEALTHY, WARM, AND CLOSE PERSONAL RELATIONSHIP WITH THEM?

The process of developing a healthy independence from parents must begin in early childhood, with the parents being responsible for the initial trend toward their child's developing responsible independence. The child must be allowed, and sometimes required, to do things for himself, such as dressing himself, and tying his shoelaces. As he grows older, he must be allowed to make some decisions on his own and to have those decisions respected by his parents. In return for the right to make personal decisions, he must shoulder the responsibility for the decisions he makes.

Across the years many experiences will develop self-confidence and gradual independence. Some examples are: spending the first night away from home with close friends, attending summer camp for a week, attending meetings of youth groups, such as Sunday school classes, choir groups, scouts, etc. Youth group discussions led by a skillful leader can develop self-expression and self-confidence. At home a young person can be taught to share in the household duties and enjoy this interfamily relationship. Early in life he or she can be led to earn his own spending money and taught to open a savings account and be proud of it. This is done through paper routes, mowing lawns, baby-sitting, and other part-time or summer jobs.

In the meantime, a healthy interpersonal relationship between parents and their children develops. The parents are proud of their children and show it through compliments and praise. A child whose parents help him to be self-sufficient and independent will appreciate his parents and shower his love on them.

One parent said, "You teach your children to walk so they can walk away from you." This is the way it ought to be. This is the nature of reality. One of the oldest documents in history exhorts parents to prepare for this when it says, "Therefore shall a man *leave* his father and mother, and shall *cleave* to his wife . . ." (Genesis 2:24, italics mine).

A little baby one year old is sweet and darling. But what parent would want to keep him at that stage in life forever? We are born to grow, to develop, to make total personal progress, and to develop a healthy independence.

Some reader may be asking, "Why do some never develop self-sufficient independence?" The problem is generally parental neglect or parental overprotection or domination. I remember counseling a twenty-five-year-old male student whose parents were paying all his college expenses, furnishing him an automobile, and giving him $100 per month spending money. He was constantly quarreling with his parents and begging for more money. Poor boy; he had been allowed to do as he pleased. Here was a twenty-five-year-old, but he was still a big baby, and his insecure parents were still trying to live his life for him. It was a sad case, indeed. On the other hand, as a college professor, my life has been blessed by observing many students who insisted on paying most or all of their own way through college, and these students normally reflected a healthy personal relationship with their parents.

We must not be afraid of the concept that children should gradually develop self-confidence and a healthy independence from parents nor assume that to do so drives a wedge between them and their parents. The opposite is true. In many ways the child becomes closer to the parent and the parent closer to the child when this relationship occurs. Their future relationships with their parents and in-laws are characterized by the warm personal glow of reciprocal trust, respect, and pride.

THE DATING PROBLEMS OF A SEVENTEEN-YEAR-OLD GIRL —AN EXAMPLE.

During the early- and middle-teen years it is easy for conflict to rise between teenagers and their parents. As we have already seen, both the teenagers and their parents share some of the responsibility for the conflict. The teenage-parent conflict is illustrated by this letter I received from Helen.

> I am a seventeen year old girl. My parents make me work at home all the time. I really don't mind it. I actually like to work. My problem is, on the weekend when I want to go somewhere, they will not let me. When they do let me go on a date I have to be back by dark. I got my driver's license when I was sixteen, and they will not let me drive by myself. What is your opinion of such strict parents, and at what time should a seventeen year old girl be in from a date?

Usually in the elementary and junior high schools, students have a certain amount of inner security. But when they enter high school, social change may come as a big shock. It seems to be a whole new ball game. Some parents panic. They try *so hard* to do right, that it turns out all wrong.

Helen's parents should have prepared themselves for this new ball game in advance. Parents ought to train their children from childhood in the direction of courtship and marriage. A mother should say to her eight-year-old daughter, "Sweetheart, you won't be with us always. You will grow up to be a lady, get married, and have children of your own."

By now, Helen's parents should have given her wise guidance on sex education and courtship. Sometimes strict, dominating, yet well-meaning parents condition their children against love, sex, courtship, marriage, and life. This is sad, indeed.

It is obvious that Helen is in very angry conflict with her parents. It is good that she likes to work. Anyone who likes to work is sure to have some other fine qualities. I have a feeling that Helen is ordinarily too fine a person to be so angry with her parents.

Let's discuss Helen's daughter-parent conflict and the time to be in from a date. Let us be objective, and see both sides of the problem.

Assuming that her parents are normal parents, and assuming that Helen has not been untrustworthy, it is obvious that her parents are too strict about her dating. A mature, seventeen-year-old girl ought to be trusted to stay out after dark to a time agreed upon by the girl and her parents. For parents to demand rigid control with an iron will over a seventeen-year-old is not good. A girl of seventeen is old enough to be trusted, yet with some limitations. For example, Helen ought to be allowed to drive her car alone to the grocery store, to the library to get books or other places she needs to go. However, Helen is too young to be given unlimited freedom with the car and allowed to fill it with friends and drive all over the country day or night at will. Some parents allow just this. I am sure teenagers will agree that some parents are not strict enough on their children. Yet, when teenagers are responsible, they should be trusted.

What are the possible reasons why Helen's parents are so strict with her? Has she abused past freedom they have given her? Does she have a habit of being disobedient? Do her parents have evidence that she has been permissive sexually with boys? Has she been associating with boys who use alcohol and/or drugs, or have a police record? Does she know that her parents are familiar with the end result of alcohol and drugs? Does she realize that her parents are acquainted with the fact of premarriage pregnancies in her community? Does she realize that some girls, given complete freedom, would go to a motel with a boy until 3:00 A.M.? Honestly now, what is the answer to these questions? If Helen's life has been a clean slate morally, and her feelings and attitudes toward other people and toward life are mature, then her parents are too strict.

Now, what can Helen do to get more freedom and heal her conflict with her parents? If there has been questionable past behavior on her part, she should apologize to her parents. She should do everything she can to stay in good communication with them. She should talk to them about her interest in boys and dating. She should ask them, kindly, for details about why they are so strict. She should let them talk. She should present her feelings and views but avoid anger and a scene. She should keep communication a two-way street. If a boy walks her home from school, she should introduce him to her parents. She should keep her parents fully informed about her courtship interests. She should try to understand that her parents are persons just as she is, and that they need love and appreciation from her. She should carefully think through the details of the sacrifices her parents have made for her during her seventeen years. She should try to understand that they love her, that they are her best friends. It is difficult for Helen to see this now, since she is in this close face-to-face relationship with her parents. But when she is older and can see things from a distance, she will probably appreciate her parents and regret some of the past conflict.

6

Engagement

WHAT IS THE BEST PROCEDURE FOR A COUPLE TO FOLLOW IN GETTING INTO ENGAGEMENT?

There are certain prerequisites to entering engagements. We will assume that John and Mary have been in a courtship relationship for approximately one year, and have been going steady for six months. She, twenty-one, and he, twenty-two, are mature for their age. They love each other and have many ideas in common. Both sets of parents approve of their courtship. Now, the question is, What is the right way to get into the relationship called "engagement"? I will be using the word engagement to mean that they both understand that they are going to be married and that this understanding is settled, finalized.

Earlier in our society it was generally understood that a couple got into engagement by way of a "proposal"; that is, John would "pop the question," asking Mary if she will marry him. In romantic literature the young lover, John, is pictured as surprising Mary by kneeling in front of her, taking her hand, and in a stirring, dramatic scene, asking if she will marry him. And in a similar dramatic scene, Mary, acting greatly surprised, accepts the proposal by saying, "Yes, John!" Only the boy could propose. And it was understood that Mary was never to hint about marriage before John "popped the question." Nonsense! Even when there was a proposal, it seldom happened the way it was portrayed in romantic literature.

The fact is that the "proposal" is fast passing into the pages of history. I made a study of courtship trends in 1966, studying the practice of three generations: (1) couples who were married in the previous five years, (2) their parents, and (3) their grandparents. Seventy-three percent of grandparents became engaged by way of proposal as compared to fifty-nine percent of parents, and only forty-seven percent of the modern generation. Thus, the proposal seems to be on the way out. As far as I am concerned, the sooner, the better.

If there is no proposal, then how do couples get into engagement? Modern young people have improved the courtship process. Thirty years ago the steps in courtship were casual dating, going steady, engagement, and marriage. Modern high school and college youth have added a new step between going steady and engagement. This new step is generally called "engaged to be engaged" and is replacing the proposal. "Engaged to be engaged" is the process in which a couple, who are going steady, begin talking in general terms about planning their lives together, gradually talking themselves into an understanding that they have tentative plans toward marriage. The understanding is usually private and personal, and is not finalized or binding. The engaged-to-be-engaged period may last for several weeks or months. During this time they continue to talk and plan. They discuss matters with their parents, and finally, they agree to a full, finalized, binding engagement. Soon after this decision, the engagement may be made public.

I personally think this new step is superior to the old, romantic-literature idea of proposal, for three reasons. (1) The boy and girl treat each other as equals as they talk about planning their lives together. The girl is brought actively into the picture. She participates in the planning dialogue, instead of coyly playing a completely passive role as she does under the old proposal system. (2) The engaged-to-be-engaged period acts like a kind of buffer zone between going steady and engagement. It tends to put off the final engagement for considerable time. Many young couples in the past have hastily moved into a full engagement too quickly. (3) Since the engaged-to-be-engaged period is not finalized or binding, it is much easier to break when necessary than an engagement. This point is important in light of the fact that we know from research that from one-third to one-half of all engagements are broken.

I recommend the new gradual, mutual, two-way-street dialogue of talking about planning two lives together as a method of getting into a finalized binding engagement. It is superior to the old "sudden, instant, patriarchal proposal" that excluded thorough mutual discussion in advance.

WHAT ARE THE THINGS THAT A COUPLE OUGHT TO DO, DISCUSS, AND PLAN TOGETHER DURING THE ENGAGEMENT PERIOD OTHER THAN PLANNING THE WEDDING CEREMONY AND HONEYMOON?

This question is far more important than most engaged couples realize. Engagement should be a happy time, not just a time to "mark time" waiting for the marriage date. It should be a time of active growth and progress, both individually and together.

During the engagement a couple ought to spend much time together planning ahead. However, do not hibernate. Continue some social activities with the same groups you associated with before engagement. During your engagement, visit each other's families as much as possible. This will be meaningful to them. Ask their advice, but make your own decisions. During engagement, accept each other as you are. There are some things about all of us that cannot be changed. Tallness or shortness can't be changed. It may be that a girl knows that in ten years her husband-to-be will be bald-headed. She will just have to love him, bald-head or hairpiece and all. If one of you is an adopted child or has grown up in a broken home, these are facts that must be understood and accepted. Accept in each other those things that cannot be changed.

During engagement teach each other your favorite games, such as tennis, bowling, golf, swimming, hiking, or chess. Try to locate and break any habits that would tend to be controversial or block future understanding. Discuss thoroughly your moral ideas, standards, ambitions, goals, and purposes in life. It would be a good planning exercise for each of you to write out privately a short paper on "What I would like for us to do together with our lives in marriage and what I think God would have us do." On a planned date read the two papers. Discuss them thoroughly, and then, after careful thought and prayer, rewrite the two papers into one paper stating, "What we would like to do with our lives together and what we think God would have us do." Keep the paper as a guide and make your plans. Most human beings do what they want to do. We might as well do that which is right and best.

Discuss money during engagement. Read the chapters on money in *Building a Successful Marriage*[1] or from other good family books in your community library. Discuss such questions as how you feel about debts, installment buying, budgets, insurance, and savings.

Also discuss what place Christianity and the Church will take in your lives. Will you attend church regularly? Will you be Sunday school teachers? Will you give a tithe of your income to your local church? Will you read the Bible and have family prayer in your home?

Discuss planned future occupation in careful detail. How will it affect your family life? Will the husband ever need to change occupations? If so, when? And, to which one? Will either of you need further education after marriage? If so, which one of you? When? How much? Under what circumstances? Does the wife-to-be plan to work outside the home for pay? If so, for how long and for what purpose?

---

[1] Judson T. Landis and Mary G. Landis, *Building a Successful Marriage*, 5th ed. (New York: Prentice-Hall, 1968).

Be sure to discuss your personal health and the health of your family backgrounds. Do not hide any health skeletons in the closet.

Discuss future roles in your home life. Who will be expected to do what? What will your social life be like in marriage? (Girls, be careful about marrying a stay-at-home type of husband. Boys, be careful about marrying a gadabout, busybody wife.) How will you make decisions as husband and wife? Who will be the final authority? If love prevails, there will be no problems here. There are no bosses in happy families.

What will be your relationship with your parents after marriage? During your engagement you both should eliminate all appearance of extreme parental attachment. You can cut "apron strings" and still love your parents.

Discuss future children. When? How many? What methods of child training will you use? Of course, you must discuss attitudes toward sex and birth control. Two weeks or two months before your wedding, read together my book *Sexual Happiness in Marriage*.[2] Discuss frankly your beliefs and feelings about sex in marriage. The discussion should be a rational understanding and exchange of ideas and not an emotional, sex-stimulating affair.

If either of you has any problems or situations that you are doubtful or uncertain about, seek counsel on these matters and clear them up in your minds as much as possible before marriage. Engagement should be a happy creative time of growth and progress for a couple, individually and together.

IS IT ADVISABLE FOR A GIRL TO MARRY A COLLEGE STUDENT WHO HAS SEVERAL YEARS OF COLLEGE AND GRADUATE WORK AHEAD, KNOWING HE WOULD BE DEPENDENT ON HER FOR FINANCIAL SUPPORT?

The answer would have to be a qualified yes and no.

[2] Grand Rapids: Zondervan Publishing House, 1967 (paperback $1.95).

If a courtship is a questionable, borderline case, the answer is no! Such a marriage would probably end in disaster. However, if the couple has experienced a sincere bona fide courtship and engagement, if they are committed to accepted Christian moral values, and if they are mature both in age and in personality development, the answer is yes, go ahead. But the details must be planned and understood in advance. The wife-to-be must be willing; she must want this arrangement.

There are three problems involved in such a marriage:

1. There is the ever-present problem of a pregnancy interrupting this educational plan. This is why most parents object to this type of marriage. The facts are that in today's world most couples *can* control birth, if they will rigidly follow contraceptive information, and they *can* at the same time have a healthy sexual adjustment. But research indicates that over one-half of college marriages have unplanned pregnancies. Doctors and marriage counselors can give couples the best information available on family planning, but they cannot make them practice it. When a couple violates rules, they are responsible for the results.

2. A second problem is the pride of mature young men in a society that still says, "The husband should be the breadwinner." Some young men "feel like a heel" in being dependent on their wives financially. This ought not to be a major objection in today's world. It is accepted for women to work outside of the home for pay. A realistic approach to this problem on the part of the young man should be somewhat as follows: In the early years of marriage, a wife works for pay while he studies and trains, often without pay. This training will pay off for both of them in the years ahead. When his graduate work is completed, he works for pay while she works in the home and helps raise the children, without pay. All that both make belongs to both of them, always, for they are partners.

Let us not overlook the fact that while the young husband is in graduate school, he is not a lazy, shiftless slug-gard. He is *working*. Graduate work is probably the hardest work he will ever do in his life.

3. The third problem is that in this wife-work-and-hus-band-study situation the husband and wife attain different intellectual and social levels. They live, think, and act in two different, isolated worlds. She does not understand his big words, nor does she enjoy the social life with his pro-fessional friends. Such a life is not satisfactory for either husband or wife. Recently I read of a man whose wife dropped out of school and worked, paying his way through an M.A. and a Ph.D. degree, after which he divorced her and married an intellectual. That man is a low-down heel, a rascal, and a scoundrel. Furthermore, he is a thief and a robber.

Normally it is better for couples entering this type of marriage to be college graduates or at least twenty-one years old. However, assuming that the prospective marriage is a *good* marriage risk, go ahead and marry with the posi-tive understanding that the wife will go to school and will stay on his educational level. One way to do this is for both of them to work half-time and both go to school half-time. I have observed several married couples who took six years (six winters and six summers) to work their way through college. The wife would work at a factory three years while the husband finished his work for a col-lege degree. Then the husband would work at the factory until she received her college degree. There are other couples where the wife financed the husband through four to seven years of college and graduate school, and then the husband "moved heaven and earth" to see to it that she got equal schooling with him.

Only under these circumstances do I recommend that the wife finance her husband's education. But I do recom-mend it for the right people and under the right circum-stances. Thousands of fine couples have followed this ar-rangement successfully.

AS THE DATE OF MARRIAGE APPROACHES, IS THE FEELING OF DOUBT ABOUT CHOOSING THE RIGHT PERSON VERY COMMON?

Yes, it is very common. Let us examine and analyze these doubts. What is their origin, their source?

Sometimes the cause of such doubts is rooted in minor and insignificant ideas. Doubts tend to show up after making major life decisions, such as choosing a college, an occupation, or making a major spiritual or moral life decision. Or, suppose a young person has been overprotected by parents who have made all of his decisions. When he has to make a major decision such as choosing a marriage companion, he might expect doubts after making his decision. Also he would expect doubts if he were a very insecure person. One may also expect some doubts as the result of just plain fear. He may have fear of the wedding ceremony. Or, there may be simple fear because, in marriage, one is traveling into a new land, a new life experience, an uncertain future, one that may bring happiness or unhappiness.

If a person has doubts as the wedding date approaches, I suggest that he have a private conference with himself and carefully examine his courtship from the very beginning. He should ask questions such as these: Has our courtship been long enough? Are we mature enough to shoulder the responsibilities of marriage? Do our parents and friends approve of this marriage? Do we have moral and spiritual values in common? Is our proposed marriage a good marriage risk? If an honest answer to these and similar questions is a positive yes, then it is obvious that his doubts are not anchored in any real reason why he should not marry. Therefore, I suggest that he go ahead and get married, even with his doubts. After he is married these doubts will disappear.

On the other hand, if when he examines his courtship, he discovers that in reality the person he is planning to marry is a person of low morals, with no ambition and no religion, is antagonistic to religion, has a mixed system of values, is insecure, is confused, or has no self-control, I would recommend that he immediately postpone the date of his marriage. Why? Because his doubts are not imaginary shadows. They are real. They are his conscience, his inner social, moral, and spiritual wisdom and better judgment warning him of the dangers ahead. In his courtship, he has been playing a trick on himself.

When doubts rest upon questionable characteristics of one's sweetheart, I suggest that the two have some long talks with each other in the hope that they may save each other as a person, and in so doing save the marriage. If one cannot succeed in this positively and confidently, then it is in order to dissolve the engagement and start over. "To thine own self be true." It is never safe to enter into an extremely questionable marriage. When in major doubt, don't.

HOW DOES ONE BREAK AN ENGAGEMENT?

From one-third to one-half of all engagements to be married are broken. Before engagement, couples usually put their best foot forward in order to impress one another. When they become engaged, they often think, *This is it! The matter is settled.* They then relax and cease past aggressive behavior. During the "let-down" period, when they take each other for granted, their real habits and attitudes of selfishness surface, and one or both realizes that the engagement was a mistake.

It is not easy to break an engagement, especially after public announcements have been made and a diamond ring is involved. But when "worst comes to worst," and an engagement has to be broken, what is the best procedure? Of course, it would probably vary according to the circumstances involved. When both parties equally agree at the same time that the engagement should be broken, then there is little or no problem. This is often the case when youth who are too young have moved into engagement too quickly. On the other hand, with courtship, major problems are involved, especially when one person does not want to break up.

How should the person breaking the engagement proceed? How can he or she sever the relationship and do the least damage? The person breaking the engagement should keep in mind that he or she has been a party to the engagement and therefore has some responsibility. He has taken up several months, a year, or more of the person's valuable time—during the period when it was normal for that person to be serious about finding a life's companion.

In my opinion, it is wrong—and cruel—for a boy (or girl) to write a surprise letter breaking the engagement, to leave town, simply to "drop out of existence," or to take a jet plane to outer Mongolia and never see his fiancée again. The person breaking the engagement should do so in such a manner as to do the least damage to the other party. One should leave the partner in the best possible position to pick up the broken pieces of his ego and life, to allow wounds to heal, and to start life and courtship over again.

One approach to a broken engagement is to allow the break to be gradual, involving a little time. On a date some hints could be dropped, such as "I am disappointed that we are not as happy during our engagement as we were in our early courtship." Or "Maybe, we need to take some time to rethink things again." In a week or so, announce that you have decided that the engagement must be broken. But before the final break, say, "I want us to take one or two weeks without seeing each other so that we can think and pray about our future." At the end of this period, ask for a conference in which you can spend one or two hours in an honest attempt to explain the real reasons why the engagement must be broken. Do so in such a way as to do the least damage to the hurt party. In the process of the break, some compliments and ego builders would be in order. However, in an attempt to be mature and kind in the process of breaking off, do not "chicken out" of your intentions, regardless of the attitudes or threats of the hurt person.

Judson and Mary Landis warn that

> the immature adult who threatens suicide when a love affair is ended against his will does so because he wishes to force the loved one to worry over him, to fear he will harm himself, and to feel responsible for his behavior. He hopes it will cause the loved one to decide she loves him too much to risk allowing him to harm himself. Sometimes in fiction, or movies, the jilted lover drinks to drown his sorrow until his former sweetheart comes back to him; then they marry happily.... If fiction pictured life situations rather than romantic fantasy, it would tell what happened later in the married life of the girl who weakened and married the man after he proved his love for her by turning to liquor. Instead of living happily ever after, she would be spending the rest of her life trying to pacify a husband who resorts to sulking, temper tantrums, or drunkenness whenever things failed to go according to his wishes. Immature patterns of behavior do not change with marriage any more than selfishness is cured by marriage.[3]

There are three acceptable rules young people should follow relative to broken engagements. (1) It is better to delay an engagement than to have to break an engagement. (2) If an engagement needs to be broken, break it. (3) It is much easier to break an engagement than to have to break a marriage.

HOW DOES ONE RECOVER FROM A BROKEN ENGAGEMENT?

It is not easy to recover from a broken engagement, especially for the "hurt" person. Yet, as I have said before, it is much better to break an engagement than to have to break a marriage.

When engagements are broken, the immature hurt person may respond by promiscuity to build up ego, by excessive drinking or the use of drugs, by threatening to

---

[3] Landis and Landis, *Building a Successful Marriage*, p. 231.

tell things that ought not be told, by threatening the life of the lover, or by threatening suicide. Usually these threats are not carried out. The mature person, although hurt deeply, will want to respond to his problem by coming to grips with reality, intelligently.

The first shock of broken engagement usually causes immediate depression. When this happens, do not repress your feelings. Go ahead and cry if you feel like it. There is a "time to weep," and this is one of those times. Discuss your breakup with an understanding parent, friend, or counselor. Buy yourself something new to give you a lift. Most important, you need to realize that time is a great healer and is on your side. When the immediate depression has subsided, face things as they are. Respond to reality! Do not live in the past. Do not drift into fantasy and daydreams about your former lover. Do not refuse to date other people, waiting for a future reconciliation. Evaluate your "ex" with an open mind. Do not overly criticize him (her). This can serve little purpose except to belittle yourself for being involved with "such a creep." Evaluate your "ex's" good qualities as well as his poor qualities. Honestly weigh and evaluate the differences in values, goals, and personalities of you and your "ex." View your breakup as a learning experience. Decide to discipline yourself to conquer this problem by looking to and properly planning the future. As a Christian, you should pray, believing that God will give you strength to live each day as an exciting new challenge. Thank Him for this learning experience. Take action to establish yourself as an individual again.

Do not listen to "our" song, nor go to "our" place. Avoid other places where the two of you were always together. Do not constantly socialize with those who were friends built around you as a couple. Do not constantly speak of your "ex." Do not see him (her) more than necessary. When you are unavoidably in contact with one another, be kind and courteous as you would to any other person of the community, but be careful to avoid any word, action, or gesture that might indicate you are still interested. If he opens the gate for further social relationships to you, close it kindly but firmly. If he sends you mail or presents, do not respond to them. If it continues, return them unopened.

Take positive action to occupy your time. Do not dwell on self-pity. Renew old acquaintances and ties. Meet new people. Take a vacation if possible and participate in sports. Develop a new hobby or renew an old one. Join that community group that you have never had time for. Become active in your church, and participate in its spiritual and social functions. Consider volunteer work in your hospital or neighborhood center. Although I do not recommend it, I once knew a student who transferred to another college in order to avoid a determined, pestering "ex." Two years later she was happily married and a much wiser person.

Date a variety of other people. Make yourself attractive and available. Be careful about getting serious again too quickly. Beware of a quick marriage on the rebound in an attempt to save face. Spite marriages will be failures. It normally takes as long to get into love the second time as the first time. Yet experience is on your side. Set your sails in the direction of a good marriage. Plan and pray to that end. Millions of others in your circumstances have moved out of disappointment into happy marriages. You can, too!

WHEN AN ENGAGEMENT IS BROKEN, WHAT IS THE PROPER PROCEDURE FOR RETURNING GIFTS?

When an engagement is broken, permanently, there are many important decisions related to the future of both that must be made. The problem of what to do with gifts can be painful and embarrassing if it is not handled graciously and tactfully.

One major guideline that should direct these decisions is the fact that both the boy and the girl are responsible for this courtship that has advanced to the stage of giving and accepting an engagement ring and making wedding plans. They both have taken up one or more important years of each other's time, often during the years when normal courtship and marriage should take place. Therefore they both should cooperate to dissolve the relationship in such a thoughtful manner that it will help each to pick up the pieces of life and start over with the least amount of trauma. This is especially true of the person terminating the engagement.

The first thing to be given back is the diamond ring. It is a symbol of a courtship bond that was to mature, but it has no meaning when that bond is broken. You no longer belong to each other. Thus the engagement ring should be returned, plus all other rings such as class rings, going steady rings, and other promise rings. To keep these rings would give your former fiancé false hope that perhaps one day things might still work out. Also, one should return all jewelry and anything that was symbolic of your belonging to each other. Return everything that is in good taste to return, such as expensive photos, one-of-a-kind snapshots, impossible-to-replace pictures, heirlooms, and any gift that has sentimental value to the giver. Pictures in which you both appear are yours; do as you please with them. Return graciously anything requested by the giver. Regardless of personal hurt, honor each other's personal requests and feelings.

Keep those things that are well used and those that were not personal to the giver. Examples are cosmetics, scarfs, gloves, sweaters (not class or letter sweaters), and inexpensive costume jewelry. Keep whatever the other requests that you keep, within reason. It is generally understood that letters and greeting cards belong to the receiver to be kept for historical purposes or disposed of as one wishes. However, if they are requested, return them, but the receiver could make and keep photostatic copies of important documents for historical purposes. Things that couples bought together belong to neither. Decide jointly what to do with them. If in doubt, an understanding of ownership should be reached between the two of you, with the holder graciously conceding to the decision.

In all decisions, treat the other person with fairness, concern, and selflessness. To belittle oneself by keeping something for spite or by destroying things of value is selfish and immature. Nothing is to be gained by hanging onto or arguing over something that no longer is symbolic of its original designation.

Return all shower gifts to the givers, unless they insist that you keep them. Dr. Evelyn Duvall says,

> The girl may return the gifts of value which can be used by someone else with a simple note telling of the change in plans and thanking the giver for his thoughtfulness. In case of such things as monogrammed linens, or other articles that have been personalized for her alone, she need do nothing except inform the giver . . . of her change in plans.[4]

SOME ENGAGEMENT DANGER SIGNALS—AN EXAMPLE

During the engagement period, many young people can become so excited in their infatuation with the happiness and blessings of engagement and the prospects of a long-planned-and-dreamed-of perfect marriage including its free and unlimited personal intimacies, that they become blinded to reason, rationality, and reality. They overlook faults and facts. They read into each other and their prospective marriage, qualities and conditions that do not exist. This is why we insist that intelligence must direct all decisions in the courtship processes. It is normal in courtship to express emotional feelings and love for each other, but emotional expressions must always be prompted and promoted by intelligence and propriety.

The following letter, received from Henry, a college graduate, illustrates how easy it is to ignore courtship danger signals.

---

[4] Evelyn Millis Duvall, *Love and the Facts of Life* (New York: Association Press, 1969), p. 312.

When I was twenty-two years old I married Sandra. She was nineteen. We had a courtship of one and a half years. She came from a good home. They were not rich, but they were not poor. She and her parents were active in church. Sandra was beautiful. She always dressed well. She was romantic and continually expressed her love for me. She looked forward to marriage. During our courtship, I dreamed of a long, happy married life with her. After marriage, we settled down in a nice apartment and both were to go to school. I was to work on a master's degree and she was to finish college. When school started, I enrolled, and she decided to wait one semester before enrolling. I worked after school five hours per day. Our marriage relationship was happy and complete, I thought.

Yet at the end of five weeks of marriage, I came home from school before going to work and Sandra was gone. She had left a note. It read, "Henry, I have gone home to Mother. Marriage is not for me now. I am doing this for my sake and yours. It will be much easier for me to do this now, than for it to happen after some children are born. My decision is final." I was shocked. I was stunned. This was impossible. In emotional shock, I grabbed the telephone and called, but she refused to talk to me. I talked to her parents, who were as shocked as I was. I did everything humanly possible to re-establish our marriage. All efforts were in vain.

Of course, it left me defeated, discouraged, and depressed. You can't love someone, as I loved Sandra, and get over it in a week or a month. As I attempted to pick up the pieces and start life over, I asked myself over and over again, what did I do wrong? Why could I have so misjudged her? As I began to face reality, I became aware of the cold sobering truth. I had responded to her physical beauty and her social gaiety. Depending on these facts, I had blindly ignored some glaring red danger signals flashing all over the place.

As an only child, her parents had loved her and had done EVERYTHING for her. They waited on her hand and foot. They bought her the best of fine clothes, and all other things a teenage girl could want. Her parents, relatives, and neighbors had constantly bragged on her beauty. She was a social high-flier with dignity, yet she reveled in it. She had never worked. She knew nothing of responsibility. She did not know how to cook nor how to accept the responsibility of a home. She was self-centered, selfish, and egotistical. She knew nothing about human values or re-spect for other people. She thought only of herself. Suc-cessful romance and social life called for marriage; so she used me as a tool. Planning the marriage and going through the social aspects of it were a joyous delight to her as a high-flying socialite.

Before our marriage, I asked my mother's advice about the marriage. Mother said cautiously, "Son, your father and I want you to be happy. If you want to marry Sandra, you have our blessing, but, frankly we are afraid that she does not have the inner personal stability necessary for a happy, successful marriage. She is not the MATURE PERSON that you need." Why, oh why, did I not heed my mother's ad-vice? I was so enthused with Sandra's physical beauty and social acceptance that in my blindness I by-passed my mother's warning, and all the other red-flashing danger signals.

Please feel free to use my experience to warn young people to consider carefully courtship danger signals before rushing to the marriage altar.

Henry

7

Special Problems Related to Courtship, Engagement, and Marriage

MUST THE BOY BE OLDER THAN THE GIRL IN COURTSHIP AND MARRIAGE?

There are two questionable ideas related to the subject of age and marriage. The first is the idea that the boy *must* be older. Our culture, going back many generations, teaches this extreme. Many other nations, including India, are even more determined about the boy being older than is our society. I suspect this idea, because it is pure tradition built upon the false idea of male superiority, male authority, and male dominance. It is blind tradition. It does not rest upon reality or facts, scientific or otherwise. Tradition may be good or bad, depending on whether or not it meets the needs of people, including both individuals and the group, and both men and women. Our cultural traditions must form a workable foundation for a healthy society. When traditions do not meet the needs of persons in society, they should be changed. However, we must not overlook the fact that many of our traditions, perhaps a majority of them, are good and do not need to be changed. Rather, they need to be reapplied to our changing, mechanized culture.

It is difficult to measure the problems, the conflicts, the havoc, and the heartaches this socially imposed rule that the man must be older (though not many years older) has foisted upon individuals (especially women) and society.

The second questionable idea is that it is acceptable for couples to marry with a major age difference such as ten to twenty years or more. Extreme age difference presents major problems of goals, values, social interaction, and conflict due to the development of feelings of superiority or inferiority. When I read about a rich old man marrying a beautiful young movie star, I suspect the motives of both of them.

There ought to be an acceptable middle ground. Ordinarily, two or three years difference in age either way makes little or no difference. Age does not mean maturity, nor does it mean having acquired the traits and habit patterns which should determine marriageability. Maturity and growth vary with individuals. Family and community backgrounds have much to do with both the maturity and growth of individuals.

Age does not coincide with physical health. A twenty-five-year-old man or woman who has followed a life of proper diet, exercise, sleep, and emotional stability can be more healthy than a boy or girl of fifteen who has not. Spiritual, social, physical, and sexual exhaustion are determined by lack of both motivation and an exciting healthy attitude, rather than by age.

There is some rather strong evidence that it is well for the girl to be two or three years older than the boy in courtship and marriage. The different rate of sexual development of the boy and girl should be considered. A boy reaches his sexual peak at approximately age nineteen, while the girl does not reach her sexual peak until approximately age twenty-nine. Many girls who marry in their early teens have some major problems in sexual adjustment in the early part of their marriage. However, the problem is not solely slower sexual development. Immaturity on the part of both the bride and the groom may be involved. Unfortunately, many such marriages end in divorce. If a girl is two or three years older than her fiancé at marriage (he is twenty-one and she is twenty-three), there should be a better possibility of early sexual adjustment in marriage. Good sexual adjustment early in marriage is healthy for any marriage.

Also, in our society, women live longer than men. Thus, if a wife is two years older, the husband would not retire earlier than his wife. The wife would not feel obligated to quit working in order to be with her husband during retirement, and would not need to forfeit any retirement benefits. Also, normally the husband and wife would approach death more nearly at the same time than otherwise. The average wife would not be left widowed for as long a period of time.

A person's personality, habit patterns, and emotional maturity are not determined by age. They are determined by such factors as (1) being needed, wanted, accepted, and loved by mature, secure parents at birth, (2) being taught self-confidence by skillful parental authority and leadership during childhood, and (3) being tenderly brought up to adulthood in the education and discipline of accepted and tested moral values.

Of course, age is one of the factors that should be considered in selecting a marriage partner, but it must be seen in the light of other mental, emotional, moral, and spiritual values.

It is true that the nearer a couple are to the same age at marriage, the better it is for their marriage. However, the idea that the boy must be older than the girl is a cultural lag. Ordinarily, two or three years difference either way presents little or no problems.

LOVE-MAKING IN PUBLIC?

To object to love-making in public is not to object to love-making at the proper time or place and with the proper understanding and restraint.

Some of the public behavior of a few couples on our high school and college campuses and in our communities is extremely embarrassing to most of the people of the community, to the high school and college faculty, and administration, and, yes, to most other students and young people. To those who wonder why some youth behave in this way, one answer is, the adults of America have taught them through TV sex scenes, X-rated movies, pulp magazines, and similar printed trash.

Public love-making labels a couple, both boy and girl, in the mind of the community. Their character and reputation are immediately obvious to all when they allow affections (?) to become a community affair. Those who pass by or "stumble over" them are usually embarrassed and offended. Small children may get the wrong idea about sex and its real meaning in life. The couple becomes a target for gossip and ridicule.

Who is responsible, the boy or the girl? Many times very immature, selfish young men have not been taught or have not learned how to control their strong sex drive. All too often it is the boy who forces the issue, and the girl goes along reluctantly. Yes, usually he is the aggressor.

If in a given situation the boyfriend publicly makes advances, the girl should first state her convictions kindly but firmly. If he continues, she should insist that he stop. She may try to change the subject or suggest other activities. If he persists, she should restate her position and leave or ask to be taken home. When all of the facts are considered, one may rightly conclude that boys are more responsible than girls for the ugly spectacle of love-making in public.

However, sometimes the girl is at fault and should share half of the responsibility or more for such behavior. Often she asks for it, even if she does so unconsciously. By her gestures, eye movements, tone of voice, body movements, the clothing she wears, and adjusting her skirt upward, she can willfully "turn on" the strong sex drive of her date.

Although the boy's sex drive is much more easily "turned on," I want it understood that I think the responsibility for such behavior should rest equally on both the boy and the girl. It needs to be said that both of them have the means, the method, and the self-control necessary to prevent love-making in public if they want to do so. In both the early and the later stages of courtship they both should be prepared with a plan. Each might well be guided by the philosophy that he has moral responsibilities to himself, to his date, to society, and to his Creator. The couple must see physical attraction and sex as important, but not as the foundation for a healthy friendship, nor the sole item of interest.

Let me repeat, some of the public behavior of a few couples in most communities is immature, extreme, disrespectful, crude, and vulgar. We all need to learn that love (1) is very personal, (2) demands privacy, and (3) loses something when it has an audience. I strongly suspect lovemaking in public as being "sex as an end in itself," as being lust, not love.

Do not assume that to object to love-making in the public is to object to all courtship love-making. There is a proper time, and a proper place. There must be proper understanding and proper restraint.

We must not confuse a "hello" kiss, after considerable absence, with exploitive courtship love-making in public. "For everything there is an appointed time; and there is a time for every purpose under the heavens . . . a time to embrace and a time to refrain from embracing" (Ecclesiastes 3:1, 5). For further reading on this topic I suggest chapter eight "How to Control Sex Until Marriage" in my book, *Sexual Understanding Before Marriage* (Zondervan, 1971).

WHAT SHOULD BE THE ATTITUDE OF THE FLAT-CHESTED GIRL AS COMPARED TO A 36-24-36?

Many young girls suffer much worry and anxiety over the shape of their bodies. The following letter from a teenage girl is a pertinent example.

I have a very personal problem that has caused me much worry. I just cannot talk to my mother about it. I am too embarrassed to talk to any of my friends about it. I do not have the courage nor the money to talk to a doctor.

I am 15 years old, five feet, four inches tall and have normal weight for my age and height. My problem is (it embarrasses me to write this) I am "flat-chested." My breasts are small, too small. I imagine boys laugh at me and that some girls reject me as a friend. I worry about whether or not I will be normal sexually in marriage.

Jane

The real question this letter is asking is, "Does a woman's body shape affect her sexual capacity in marriage?" The answer has to be an emphatic *NO!* Yet I can understand why a girl has worries about herself living in a society whose culture associates sex with body shape, as does our society. Let me explain. For many years the money-minded propaganda media, television, especially Hollywood movies, the advertising industry, and slick and "sexy" magazines, have been saying by implication that only women with a certain size and shape of body are really "sexy." Unfortunately, many men and women seem to have believed this naive propaganda. Thus, "36-24-36" has become a false symbol. This is one of the most fantastic lies that has ever been accepted by our seemingly educated but gullible public. This ridiculous "36-24-36" idea is largely an invention of men and not of women. Such men are interested in satisfying their own selfish sex drives and promote sexual permissiveness in order to make quick, easy money in their particular (often very questionable) occupation.

The late Dr. Joseph G. Molner, M.D., said, "A female can be mean, ornery, neurotic, selfish, stupid, greedy or frigid—but if she has a big bosom, she's automatically supposed to be the 'Ideal Woman.' This is tape-measure baloney!"

To say that only girls with certain body measurements can be attractive or sexy is about as intelligent as saying that all girls who are over six feet tall or under five feet tall have weak, inefficient stomachs and lungs. Or it is about as sensible as saying that the color of a woman's hair or skin determines her sexual efficiency in marriage. The size or shape of a person's body has little or nothing to do with his or her sexuality. The only exception to this is when a person becomes excessively overweight. In such cases, available energy is consumed in carrying excess body weight, and thus these people have less energy for normal sex life. The real tools for a satisfying sex life in marriage lie within a person's mind. They are such qualities as character, honesty, love, concern, fidelity, trust, thoughtfulness, tenderness, understanding, cooperation, and a balanced sex education.

There is much evidence that many other young girls worry about this problem. All of them seem to have what Keith Olson calls "a negative body image"[1] that causes them to feel insecure and inferior. To persist in this attitude is dangerous. Note the facts. Jane is very young. When she grows to adulthood, her breasts will grow larger, and she will feel that they are normal. Girls who have larger breasts at her age will tend to have breasts that are too large, that tend to sag, and that may be cumbersome in later years. Girls should respond to the truth about this problem. Every person is a unique creation of God. God has not cheated us. Jane is a normal person now. Just as all leaves are different, so all human bodies are different. I assume that Jane is in good health and has a good mind. She is not deformed. She does not have cancer. She is not a social leper. In her fears she is living in the outer fringes of life. Other Janes who read these lines should leave this shadowy twilight zone and move with positive confidence into the center of total life, so wonderfully planned for them by the Creator.

In the meantime, as life unfolds to full adulthood, maturity, and marriage, young people should be proud of their bodies! They are the "temple of the Holy Spirit."

IS THERE A RISK INVOLVED IN MARRYING A PERSON WITH A FEW MINOR BAD HABITS?

In order to discuss this question, it is necessary to de-

---

[1] *Campus Life*, October, 1972.

fine "a few minor bad habits." What do these words mean? Do they mean that a boy does not wear his coat on social occasions when most other men do? Do they mean that he wears gaudy-colored neckties? Do they mean that he uses poor English, such as "I seen him"? A young man might have this type of minor bad habit and be a good marriage risk. These habits are things that can be corrected.

However, if by "a few minor bad habits" is meant such things about a young man as that (1) he is exceedingly greedy, (2) he uses adult temper tantrums to get his way, (3) he drinks a pint of whiskey per week, (4) he gambles away his paycheck on Saturday night, (5) he can lie easier than tell the truth, (6) he proudly uses profanity to impress people of his courage, or (7) he freely violates women at will—then this question is a horse of another color.

There are two items of homespun philosophy that come tumbling into my mind as I think about this question: (1) "As a person has been, so will he be" and (2) "As life moves on, little molehills of human habits tend to grow into mountains." If a boyfriend will curse in the presence of his girlfriend before they get married, after they are married he will curse her. If a boyfriend will drink liquor before he gets married and use spices to kill the smell on his breath, after he is married he will drink twice as much, use no spices, blow his breath into his wife's face and laugh at her. Frankly, I think young people had better take a long look at these so-called "minor bad habits" before going to the wedding altar.

Every boy or girl has a right and a responsibility to marry a moral person. After marriage we must live in a society that is trying to be moral. And the best time for a girl or boy to do any moral reforming of a sweetheart is before marriage. Before marriage your position, your level of efficiency, is much more effective. I suspect a promise that one will stop "minor bad habits" after marriage. Can we be sure the habits will stop? A young person should do all of his reforming before he arrives at the marriage altar. And be sure that it is genuine reformation and not just an empty promise in order to get through the marriage ceremony.

I can hear some objectors say, "Does one have a right to demand that his or her sweetheart change his or her life completely to fit the moral ideals of the other? Does not the individual have any rights?" Yes, the individual has rights, but there are two individuals involved in marriage. Both have rights. When a moral person marries an immoral person, neither may expect happiness because the one's habits of immorality will eventually destroy them. In marriage both partners should allow one another to remain individuals, free, within limits, to grow and develop toward self-fulfillment. Love and marriage demand that each assist the other in that direction. I can hear the objector ask, "Within what limits?" One wise answer would be, "Within the limits of the Ten Commandments." Those people who object to moral limits overlook three things: (1) There is abundant evidence that happiness results when two moral people love and marry each other; (2) those who continue to violate moral rules eventually destroy themselves; and (3) moral rules are not our enemies but are our strong, zealous, ardent friends. My pastor reminds us that the fence around the kindergarten playground is not the children's enemy and it is not there to take away their freedom. It is there to protect them so they can be free to play unharmed. Moral laws are not enemies to steal our freedom; they are friends to protect us from our self-centeredness and thus give us freedom to develop happiness in marriage and life. Young people should deal honestly and forthrightly with these so-called "few minor bad habits" before marriage. To marry without doing so may turn out to be taking a *giant step backwards*.

SHOULD COURTING COUPLES CONFESS PAST "SKELETONS IN THE CLOSET" TO ONE ANOTHER BEFORE GOING TO THE MARRIAGE ALTAR? IF SO, WHEN?

Sue was to be married to Ron in about two months.

She was very happy and was looking forward to her new life with him. As the date of the marriage approached, her conscience began to bother her, as she wondered if she should "confess" an earlier experience to Ron.

About three years earlier (before she met Ron) Sue worked as a secretary in a law firm. There were several young lawyers there, and she had been interested in one of them. One night they both had to work late. When he offered to drive her home, she accepted. After a few minutes of driving, it became evident to Sue that he was not taking her home. She told him this, but he just kept driving. She begged him to stop, but instead he drove even faster. It was obvious that he was taking her to a well-known secluded "parking place" for lovers. He stopped the car, and began making passes at Sue. She screamed and tried to get away, but he was stronger than she. By this time, she was screaming and crying frantically. A policeman, making his regular rounds, heard her cries for help. He rushed over and arrested the young lawyer. It was a very traumatic experience for Sue, but she had almost forgotten it until she started making marriage plans.

Uncertain as to whether she should tell Ron, she went to her pastor for advice. Her pastor suggested that she should tell Ron and assured her that she had not been at fault, because the young lawyer was the aggressor. He had willfully trapped her. He used force. Sue had no evil intentions and had desperately tried to repel him. He had not succeeded in raping her. Her original traumatic experience was now a dim memory. Certainly Ron would understand and his love for her would increase.

But not all past "skeletons-in-the-closet" are as easily handled as Sue's problem.

There is no easy yes-or-no answer to the question of "confessing the past" during courtship, but there are some guidelines that should be helpful.

1. You should not confess past problems during the early dating period. During this period of casual dating

the relationship is one of getting acquainted, developing social proficiency, learning to understand self and those of the opposite sex. Usually young people date several different people during the casual dating period. To discuss personal and intimate details about one's past hardly belongs to this level of courtship.

2. The responsibility of confessing one's past behavior belongs to the "going steady" period of courtship, when marriage is being considered. This is the period in which couples study each other seriously. They are interested in each other's spiritual, educational, social, and occupational goals. They are concerned about family and community backgrounds. They consider each other's life philosophy, moral values, and spiritual commitment. It is obvious that any confessing of the past that must be done belongs to this courtship period.

3. Do not wait until engagement to confess past behavior, for your sweetheart may feel he or she has been deceived. In some cases it leads to broken engagements.

4. Certainly one should not wait until after marriage to confess the past. The deception and emotional problems can become acute and critical in the marriage relationship. There are much greater problems in breaking a marriage than in breaking an engagement.

5. In most cases, sweethearts should wait for each other to volunteer to tell about past questionable behavior. For either to snoop and pry into the other's past life by insinuations, implications, and questions is, at best, very bad taste.

6. Dr. and Mrs. Judson Landis state that couples should carefully consider four questions before doing any confessing: (1) Why do I feel I must tell? (2) Will our marriage be happier if I do tell? (3) Will my fiancé(e) be happier if I tell? (4) If I must tell, is my fiancé(e) the best person to tell it to? In some cases, they suggest that it might be better to do the confessing to a clergyman or a marriage

counselor "who can remain silent, and undisturbed and is capable of giving wise counsel."[1]

7. There are some things that must be told before engagement and marriage. This would include the presence of disease, hereditary defects, a previous marriage, a child born out of wedlock, major debts, a venereal disease, a homosexual tendency, a prison record, and serious police records. These are things that are known by other people and usually cannot be kept secret. The facts will surface sooner or later.

8. Finally, I am persuaded that, when all things are considered, premarital sexual intercourse should be told before engagement. One problem is the fact that boys talk, and girls talk. It is better for your sweetheart to hear it from you, than from someone else. My research shows that 83% of church-related college students feel that questionable past sexual behavior should be discussed with the fiancé(e) before engagement and marriage. The honest approach is superior to going into marriage without bringing the matter up. To keep silent means the guilty party may live with secret guilt feelings and may feel forced to tell it later after marriage, which usually involves a major period of emotional adjustment. Yet, if Judeo-Christian attitudes are followed, the emotional upset after a premarriage confession of the past can be resolved through forgiveness and understanding, and a happy marriage can follow. However, unfortunately, in the sight of society, "the bird with the broken pinion never soars as high again."

The very fact that there is a major problem involved in whether to tell your fiancé(e) or not is another of the many reasons why young people should avoid premarital sex relations.

WHAT ARE THE PROBLEMS INVOLVED IN MARRIAGE BEFORE OR AT THE TIME OF HIGH SCHOOL GRADUATION?

---

[1] Judson T. Landis and Mary G. Landis, *Building a Successful Marriage*, 5th ed. (New York: Prentice-Hall, 1968), pp. 241, 242.

Let us look at some of the problems. (1) Those youth who marry in the middle and late teens are forced to skip much of the natural life period known as adolescence and youth. They miss the fun, the play, the frolic, the capers of those happy years. One cannot have both early marriage and a normal teenage youth. (2) The teen groom is forced to go to work, and his inexperience forces him to the bottom of the labor force. He seldom rises above it. During a rise of unemployment he is first to be discharged. The couple are generally in financial suffering. (3) A high percentage of teen marriages are followed quickly by pregnancy. This brings increased financial burdens and ties the couple down with the continuous routine of child care, which turns out to be a long, trying experience too large for many teens. (4) The long hours of work to make a living and the responsibility of child care blocks further education. The dreams of a good education on the part of the couple, and their parents' dreams for them are often shattered. (5) Their new marriage responsibilities block normal social life. There is neither time nor money for social life. They do not fit the social life of their single friends nor of older married couples. Thus the former happy high school teenagers wake up to a married social vacuum. (6) These problems are a crushing blow to their inner self-confidence. They tend to become disgusted with life. The strain is great. The young husband becomes restless. The young wife is lonely. Romance is gone. Dull boredoms set in as romantic fantasy fades. (7) Often the driving motive for teen marriages is a dream of perfect sexual ecstasy in marriage. Teen marriage circumstances are a major roadblock to normal sex life. This problem is further intensified by the fact that when a baby is born, the doctor may order no sexual intercourse for a period of four to six months and by the fact that many teenage brides are slow in sexual adjustment. Thus, both partners are emotionally wounded and frustrated. (8) In the midst of frustration and defeat the young husband often renews friendship with premarriage chums and spends much time away from home. With his strong sex drive, he often seeks promiscuous satisfaction. Or the lonely young bride seeks love and sex expression elsewhere.

In addition to these major problems, let me call attention to some other ideas that are pertinent. When young people graduate from the eighth grade, they are fourteen and are, on the average, seven or eight years away from normal maturity and marriage age. At sixteen they are still five or six years away. Girls in our society live to an average age of seventy-four. If they wait until they are about twenty-one to marry, they will still have, on the average, fifty-three years of married life. What's the hurry? Most teenagers overestimate their own maturity. All life takes time for growth. It cannot be hurried.

People of high school age have some major misconceptions about courtship and marriage, such as that love at first sight is the ideal love, the right person will come along, there is a one and only, one can depend on the marriage partner in all circumstances, sexual happiness is instantaneous, and our present personal love interests will remain permanent. Until personality patterns are more mature and stabilized, youth are unlikely to understand themselves and others. They are less likely to make a rational decision and a thorough study of what is right and what is best for them in marriage. They are more prone to marry hastily.

We must not forget that most parents usually object to early marriages, and this can set up an unhappy in-law relationship that may take years to heal. Furthermore, young people who marry in the teens tend to rob their children of mature, efficient, care and parental leadership during these crucial preschool years. It is very difficult for personality, spiritual and moral values, and emotional maturity to grow under teen-marriage circumstances.

These circumstances are the "stuff that divorces are made of." In teen marriages, usually everybody involved gets hurt: the girl bride first, her baby, her parents, the boy groom, and then friends, in that order. A teen marriage can turn sour and sad very quickly.

To be fair, some teenage marriages do survive. Yet, those involved often regret their early marriage and feel cheated out of many happy adolescent and youth experiences. And only the strong survive. *The risk is too great.*

SHOULD PARENTS HELP SUPPORT THEIR MARRIED CHILDREN FINANCIALLY?

There is no easy "yes" or "no" answer to this question. Young people living in the United States have a problem. They live in a society that calls for education through high school and college and beyond, if possible, and a very high standard of living. Yet even in this type of culture, I feel that the advantages are on the side of a couple being financially responsible after marriage, for the following reasons:

1. The Christian Scriptures seem to advocate financial independence after marriage. The couple are to "leave" their parents, "cleave" to each other, and become a single family unit (Genesis 2:24). This implies that a marriage is to be independent financially.

2. Financial independence tends to promote self-confidence, competence, and marriage success.

3. When parents disapprove of a marriage, their disapproval becomes more entrenched if they are expected to dole out money to keep the marriage going. There will follow conflicts and arguments. Conflicts and arguments are the crutches of lame minds.

4. An American rural proverb says that "the man who pays the fiddler calls the tune." When parents pay to keep the marriage going they will be tempted to tell their children how to spend their money, what decisions to make, and how to raise their children. This may lead to an impossible in-law situation.

5. Financial aid from parents can turn out to be a crutch; ambition will decline. The young couple may expect the initial gifts to become a dole or an annuity.

6. In a society where the husband is supposed to "bring home the bacon," his honor and his male ego may be crushed in his dependence on in-laws for financial help.

7. Some emotionally insecure dependent parents may freely give financially in order to hold onto their children and bolster their own sagging self-confidence.

8. A young couple's financial dependence can easily turn into emotional dependence.

Financial independence for newly married couples ought to be the rule, even in our fast-changing culture. However, there may be exceptions to the rule. An unexpected emergency may arise in the life of a young couple. It is right for loving parents to step forward and offer financial help in the crisis. It is usually best to have the understanding that the money will be repaid, preferably without interest, when circumstances permit. Or parents can help their married children by giving them gifts of money or needed merchandise as gifts on birthdays and Christmas. This promotes love and protects the ego and the independence of the couple. I recommend these exceptions. However, exceptions to the rule do not repeal the rule. It is far better for young engaged couples to save their money, plan well occupationally and economically, and even put off their marriage date for a few months, a year, or until they graduate from college in order to enter marriage in economic independence and enjoy a happy marriage in privacy, responsibility, self-confidence, individuality, and freedom.

HOW DOES OBESITY AFFECT COURTSHIP?

There are many problems that tend to block the happiness of youth during their courtship years. A considerable number of fine young people have the problem of obesity. Being overweight often causes much insecurity and anxiety as is illustrated in the following letter:

> **Dr. Miles, I am ready to graduate from high school. I make good grades. I want to go to college. Also I would**

like to date some boys and eventually get married and have a family. My problem is that I am five foot three inches tall and am sixty pounds overweight. As a result, in high school I have been a nobody. I am never asked for dates. I have no close friends. If I can pun, through my tears, I am really a big "odd" ball. What can I do that might help me out of this miserable situation?

First, one must understand that the main problem is eating *too much* and eating the *wrong kind* of food. Why do we eat too much? Basically, the reason is habit, a mental and emotional habit. In his book *The Fat Is in Your Head*,[2] Dr. Charles W. Shedd says there is a spiritual and psychological approach to overweight. Dr. Shedd, a Disciples of Christ clergyman and family life author, was 120 pounds overweight fifteen years before he wrote the book. Through spiritual and psychological insights he took off his overweight and has kept it off. The book describing his experience, consists of forty devotionals, each including a Scripture, a discussion, and a prayer.

Youth with an overweight problem would do well to secure a copy of Dr. Shedd's book, read it through and then read one devotional per day for forty days. The following quotes are selected from his book.

A hundred million Americans weigh too much. Thirty million say they are obese. If we carry 10 percent more weight than we should we are overweight; 20 percent classifies us obese. For each five pounds above ideal weight, life expectancy is reduced about one year.... He, the obese person, must view himself as his worst enemy.... We must mount guard and lie in constant ambush against ourselves. ... God only knows what sins have been committed by fat Christians at church dinners.... There is no easy way to reduce.... Self-research may be our best approach.... I tried to get a lean body on a fat mind.... Before we can get the fat off our framework, we must get it out of our heads.... Flabby waistlines mean there has been some flabby thinking.... We must surrender our phony self-image. The overweight mind forever plays tricks.... The heart suffers as it is required to pump blood through an additional

[2] Published by Word Books, Waco, Texas, 1972.

two-thirds of a mile of blood vessels for every pound of fat added. All fatties are prone to want something for nothing. . . . Those earliest food attitudes in our homes are worth studying. Looking back is unhealthy (blaming the past) when we should be moving forward. . . . Our attitudes toward our history are more important than the history. . . . Exercise is no substitute for right eating. . . . The shape we are in TALKS. . . . Sometimes, how we look cancels what we say. . . . He [Paul] quits judging others and calls himself chief of the bad guys. "For a man's ways are before the eyes of the Lord, and he watches all his paths" (Proverbs 5:21 RSV). Including the path to the refrigerator, the bakery, the malt shop, the vending machine. The purest honesty is honesty with God. I believe in the power of the mind over the body.

The book has one weakness. It hammers away at the inner spiritual and psychological feelings and gives little or no help in practical suggestions as to what to eat or not to eat. Let me make the following ten nutritional suggestions.

1. Eat beef, fish, poultry, and eggs. (The meat should be boiled, baked, or broiled.)

2. Eat vegetables, such as beets, cabbage, carrots, celery, corn, lettuce, beans, peas, and potatoes.

3. Eat fruits (uncooked when possible), such as bananas, apples, oranges, grapefruit, peaches, and pears.

4. Eat dairy products, including milk, cheese, and butter.

5. Eat small-grained foods such as whole wheat, wheat germ, oats, rice, nuts, and sunflower seeds.

6. Avoid animal fat and all types of foods cooked or fried in grease.

7. Avoid foods composed largely of starch (carbohydrates), heavy with rich, fat-producing calories such as cakes, pies, and desserts.

8. Fresh foods grown from your garden are superior; nature knows best.

9. Eat breakfast like a *king* (a large, nutritious breakfast), the noon meal like a *prince* (an average meal), and the evening meal like a *pauper* (a small meal). To eat thus will help one to lose weight. To reverse the process, as

we do in our gluttonous society, we gain weight on the same amount of food.

10. Self-understanding, self-discipline, and self-control are the keys to a full, complete, happy life.

Obesity not only limits a person's courtship possibilities, but it limits self-confidence, personality development, mental health, physical health, marriage happiness, sexual efficiency, and length of life. It is much easier to overcome obesity during the teen years than in later adult life. The time to conquer overweight is now, during your youth. Overweight young people should *admit to themselves* that they are overweight and request help from their parents, a medical doctor, the school guidance counselor, or other qualified counselors. To accept outside advice willingly and gladly is a must, but in the final analysis, it is the iron will of the obese person that must conquer the problem. There are no shortcuts. One should avoid highly advertised quick, easy cures. They are fraudulent and worthless. Remember the rule: *Eat the right amount and the right kind of food.* To reduce one's weight to the standard weight for a person of your age, height, and body frame and keep it there can lead to abundant rewards, including improved health, personality, and, yes, courtship and marriage happiness.

HOW CAN YOUNG PEOPLE WHO THINK THEY ARE UGLY KEEP THEIR PROBLEM FROM BLOCKING NORMAL COURTSHIP?

Many teenagers go through a stage of thinking they are ugly. This colors their feelings, destroys their self-confidence, develops pessimism, and may eventually adversely affect their personality. The following letter is an example of such thinking.

> **I am desperately in need of some help. To get to the point quickly, my problem is that I am UGLY. I want to associate with girls. I want to date, and eventually want to get married and have a home and some children. But girls avoid me because I'm ugly. I am seventeen years old**

and a junior in high school. I have never had a date. I have no talents. Although I am healthy and make B's in my highschool grades, I am not really good at anything. I know I need someone to help me, but do not have the courage to talk to anyone about my problem. I thought maybe you could help me.

                                          Jeff

Note Jeff's good qualities. He is in good health and must have a good mind, since he makes good grades. There are thousands of young people who would give anything for his good health, or to be able to make B's in school.

The opposite of "ugly" is "beautiful" or "handsome." Ugliness and beauty are relative terms; that is, no two people agree on what is ugly or beautiful. In our society we tend to exalt and overrate physical beauty. So-called physical beauty is lavishly and gaudily displayed on TV, in the movies, and in slick magazines with great gusto. Unfortunately, teen peer groups tend to be trapped by this physical emphasis, and many fine young people are caught in the trap.

Youth who reject themselves because they think they are ugly are overlooking several facts: (1) Facial defects such as birthmarks, acne, buckteeth, crossed eyes, or droopy ears can largely be corrected by doctors, dentists, ophthalmologists, and plastic surgeons. (2) Most people who think they are ugly have none of these problems. (3) Some people seem to identify physical ugliness with "evil," and "Hollywood beauty" with goodness. This is false. Beauty is as beauty does. (4) Many so-called ugly people develop the ability to laugh at their physical defects and turn them into an asset rather than a liability. Abraham Lincoln was everything but handsome. During the Lincoln-Douglas debates in Illinois, Senator Douglas accused Lincoln of being "two-faced." Lincoln pointed to his face and said, "It's the face my Maker gave me and, for better or for worse, the only one I have. Now do you think I would go around holding it up in front of you if I had another one?" The audience applauded his humor. Jimmy Durante laughed about his big "schnozzola" until it made him into a warm, lovable personality. (5) Our Creator-God created us as we are. "Everything God made is good, and is meant to be gratefully used, and not despised" (1 Timothy 4:4 *Phillips*). This idea of ugly vs. beautiful is a selfish human invention. I doubt if our Creator is pleased with the stupid idea that physical beauty is superior. (6) Many (not all) people with so-called physical beauty have hideous, ill-tempered, and repulsive personalities. They are self-centered, egotistical, and "camera-ready."

Now, what can young people do to solve this problem? Others may help you but *you* must tackle the problem yourself. (1) Our inner attitudes, feelings, and values are more important than external physical appearance. Positive inner attitudes can conquer most problems of external appearance. (2) Your negative self-image is unfair and unrealistic. You must stop underselling yourself to yourself. You are cheating yourself. (3) Come out of your shell. You have been secretly living inside of your self-pity with the door shut and locked. By trying to hide your feelings of inferiority, you are sealing off the approval from others that you so badly want and need. (4) Accept yourself as you are. Begin with your good gifts and qualities (a good home, good health, a good mind) and develop others. All of us have many hidden, undeveloped talents. (5) Concentrate on other people. Give compliments, be kind, smile. Be cheerful and jolly. To have friends, you must be friendly. (6) Ask for a private conference with your high school guidance counselor, with a teacher in whom you have confidence, or your pastor. They will gladly help you and keep the conference in professional confidence.

8
The Pros and Cons of Sex During Courtship

HOW SHOULD YOUNG PEOPLE RESPOND TO THE CURRENT SEX REVOLUTION?

The American family is experiencing a major sexual crisis that has not originated within the family circle but is largely the result of external ideas and forces originating from a drifting, decaying culture. A sexual revolution is here! It is real! This social and moral anarchy could annihilate our civilized family and community organization. *Never does mankind dig its own grave so deep as when it worships sex as a god and ignores the total rights and needs of persons and the plan of the Creator for their lives.*

A moral counterattack must be waged by our homes, our schools, and our churches. It must be skillful, determined, courageous, and divinely led. It must be immediate! The hour is late!

Our young people need to play a major role as the leaders in this moral counterattack. They need to understand and accept some basic truths about sex and use them as guidelines in planning courtship, marriage, and life and in directing their counterattack on sexual immorality. The following eleven simple truths are suggestive:

1. Sex is central in all of our lives, both male and female, religious and nonreligious.

2. Sex is both mental-emotional-spiritual and biologi-

cal; yet the former is more significant in normal sexual fulfillment in life than the latter.

3. Sex is a strong drive in both men and women. The Creator created it this way. Each person should admit this to himself. There is no reason why we should be ashamed of our strong sex drive.

4. Sexuality is only one aspect of total human personality. Other aspects include the spiritual, the mental, the emotional, the social, the moral, and the aspirational, to name a few. True sexual expression involves all of the aspects of personality. It is integration of all these aspects of personality that makes life complete, good, and beautiful.

5. It is easy to overstress and exploit the sexual aspect of personality and neglect the other aspects. To do so is to develop a lopsided, twisted, and perverted personality.

6. The nature of true love, sex, and the total aspects of human personality calls for monogamy in the male-female relationships, that is, one man and one woman living together permanently.

7. The personal and intimate nature of sex demands modesty in social relationships and privacy in sexual relationships.

8. One, but only one, of the major purposes of sex is reproduction. Those who reject this purpose defy one of the major purposes of human nature.

9. Sexual pleasure in marriage was planned as a means to an end, and never as an end in itself. Ultimately, the purpose of sexual pleasure in marriage was planned to bind husband and wife together in a lifelong love relationship. This lifelong love relationship was planned to provide the proper home environment for growing children.

10. Sex is difficult for growing children to understand. Therefore we need an efficient program of sex education in the home, the church, and the school.

11. The basic guidelines for sexual morality are fre-

quently, firmly, and frankly stated in the Bible and are verified by historical experience and scientific research.

WHAT ARE THE BIBLICAL TEACHINGS ABOUT SEX?

There are many clear, positive teachings about sex in the Bible. Let us list twelve of them as examples.

1. Sex is God's idea. He planned, designed, and formed the idea. Then in the beginning He created "male and female." "So God created man [human beings] in his own image . . . male and female created he them" (Genesis 1: 27). This is the first reference to sex.

2. Sex is to be practiced within marriage. "And Adam knew Eve his wife [had sex relations with her], and she conceived and bore Cain" (Genesis 4:1). The seventh commandment, stated positively, says, "Thou shalt practice sexual intercourse only within marriage." This idea is stated many times in the Scriptures: Genesis 2:18; Proverbs 18:22; Matthew 19:6; Mark 10:7-9; 1 Corinthians 5:1, 2; 6:13; 6:18; 7:9; Ephesians 5:31; 1 Thessalonians 4:3-7.

3. Sex is a uniting experience between husband and wife. "Therefore shall a man leave his father and mother, and shall cleave unto his wife: and they shall be one flesh" (Genesis 2:24). The term "one flesh" refers to sexual intercourse, which is both a physical and a spiritual experience. Thus, a man and his wife are completely united and fused into one unit. They fulfill each other's total needs. Thus, marriage becomes a reality. Jesus repeated and emphasized this one-flesh relationship (Matthew 19:5; Mark 10:7-9). Sex is something more than the union of two bodies. It is the total union of two persons.

4. Sex is primarily an experience of giving. This does not eliminate the desire to receive. "The husband should *give* to his wife her conjugal (sexual) rights, and likewise the wife to her husband" (1 Corinthians 7:3 RSV, italics mine). The husband meets his wife's sexual needs, and the wife meets her husband's sexual needs, and the one-

flesh relationship is accomplished. The word "give" means "to give over to," "to surrender to." Thus in Christian marriage, behind locked doors, in personal privacy, modesty yields and surrenders to complete abandonment and self-giving, and the unitive joy of possessing each other is realized.

5. Sex is planned by the Creator as a personal pleasure in marriage. It is the apex, the zenith, the highest height and the deepest depth of human pleasure. In the context of warning against immorality, the writer of Proverbs tells young men, "Rejoice in the wife of your youth. . . . Let her affection fill you at all times with delight, be infatuated always with her love" (Proverbs 5:18, 19 RSV). This poetic language refers to personal sexual pleasure in marriage. The Lutheran Family Life Committee rightly said that "the sheer delight of sex in marriage is the dominant theme" of the Song of Solomon. To shy away from personal sex pleasure in marriage is to miss the biblical meaning of "one flesh."

6. Sex provides husband and wife with a communicative language above and beyond words. "And Adam *knew* Eve his wife, and she conceived . . ." (Genesis 4:1, italics mine). Joseph *"knew* her not [did not have sexual relations with her] till she had brought forth her firstborn son . . ." (Matthew 1:25, italics mine). This word "know" means "to know thoroughly by experience." Sex reveals a special knowledge to a wife about her husband and herself. It reveals a special knowledge to a husband about his wife and about himself. It expresses the full meaning of love, the full meaning of male and female.

7. In the plan of God, sex is *good*. "And God saw every thing that He had made [including male and female], and, behold, it was very good" (Genesis 1:31). Paul, in criticizing people who forbade marriage, said, "For everything created by God is good and nothing is to be rejected if it is received with thanksgiving" (1 Timothy 4:4).

8. Sex is creative. "And God blessed them [Adam and Eve], and God said unto them, Be fruitful, and multiply,

and replenish the earth ..." (Genesis 1:28). The birth of a child is called "procreation," that is, creation for and on behalf of another. In sex life, husband and wife, as God's agents, are continuing His creative work. They are partners with God in creation.

9. In marriage, sex for pleasure and sex for reproduction are related, yet they are *two separate systems* with *two separate functions* in God's plan. When the Bible talks about the one-flesh marriage, referring to sexual relationship for pleasure, it says nothing about reproduction. This is true in the book of Genesis and in the writings of Jesus and Paul. Nowhere does the Bible say that sex is for the purpose of reproduction only. Whereas reproduction can occur only once in every ten or more months, the one-flesh relationship is not so limited. (It is reasonable to expect that the one-flesh sexual relationship in marriage will occur every two to four days.)

10. The one-flesh sexual relationship in marriage should glorify God. Paul was criticizing the Corinthians for sexual immorality and said, "Your body is the temple of the Holy Spirit which is in you ... therefore glorify God in your body ..." (1 Corinthians 6:19, 20).

11. The misuse and abuse of sex is evil. Jesus not only accepted and repeated the seventh commandment "Thou shalt not commit adultery" (Exodus 20:14), but He made adultery to be an inner motive when he said, "Whosoever looketh on a woman to lust after her hath committed adultery with her already in his heart" (Matthew 5:28). Paul compares adultery, fornication, and uncontrolled lust with idolatry, murder, and drunkenness and states that those who do such things shall not inherit the kingdom of God. (1 Corinthians 6:9, 10 and Galatians 5:19-21). He exhorts Timothy, "Keep thyself pure" (1 Timothy 5:22) and to control his "turbulent desires" (2 Timothy 2:22 *Phillips*).

12. All sexual sins may be forgiven. Where man's sexual sins are "stacked up high," God's forgiving grace is "stacked up much higher." "Though your [sexual] sins be as scarlet,

they shall be as white as snow ..." (Isaiah 1:18). "As far as the east is from the west, so far hath He removed our [sexual] transgressions from us" (Psalm 103:12). "He [God] will have compassion upon us ..." and will "cast all our sins into the depths of the sea" (Micah 7:19). "I [God] will forgive their iniquity, and I will remember their sin no more" (Jeremiah 31:34).

God's forgiveness is automatic, immediate, and complete. When we repent of any sin, including all sexual sins, and ask for forgiveness, in God's sight we are as if the transgression had never happened. When God forgives us of sexual sins, we ought to forgive ourselves; and relatives, friends, neighbors, and society ought to forgive us.

DOES THE BIBLE DISCUSS PREMARITAL SEX?

It is often called to our attention that some outstanding Bible scholars state that the Bible does not discuss premarital sex relations, and that Christianity has no scriptural foundation for objecting to premarital sex relations. These firm, positive statements puzzle young people in the light of their family and church backgrounds. The best approach to these statements is to examine the New Testament carefully.

The word "fornication," a translation of some form of the Greek "porneia," appears forty-seven times in the New Testament (KJV). The word translated "fornication" has four possible meanings in the New Testament. Let us examine these meanings.

1. In 1 Corinthians 7:2 and 1 Thessalonians 4:3, Paul is warning unmarried people against the temptation to fornication. In both cases he advocates marriage to prevent a single life of sexual immorality. In both cases fornication has to mean voluntary sexual intercourse of an unmarried person with anyone of the opposite sex. In four passages fornication is used in a list of sins that includes "adultery" (Matthew 15:19; Mark 7:21; 1 Corin-

thians 6:9; Galatians 5:19. Since adultery involves a married person, the word "fornication" in these passages has to mean voluntary unchastity of unmarried people.

2. In two passages (Matthew 5:32; 19:9) fornication is used in a broader sense as a synonym for adultery.

3. In some passages, fornication is used in a general sense referring to all forms of unchastity (John 8:41; Acts 15:20, 29; 21:25; Romans 1:29; 1 Corinthians 5:1; 6:18; 2 Corinthians 12:21; Ephesians 5:3).

4. In other passages, fornication refers to harlotry and prostitution, e.g., Revelation 2:14, 20, 21.

Since fornication has several shades of meaning, its meaning must be determined by the context of each passage. *Note that possibly unmarried people are included in the meanings of the word "fornication" in all of these passages where it refers to adultery, immorality, and harlotry.* Out of seven lists of evils appearing in the writing of Paul in KJV, the word "fornication" is included in five of them (2 Corinthians 5:11; 6:9; Galatians 5:19; Ephesians 5:3; Colossians 3:5) and it is first on the list each time. In Matthew 5:28, Jesus not only included sexual intercourse of unmarried people in His interpretation of adultery, but He was saying that sexual intercourse of unmarried people was as evil as extramarital sexual intercourse.

Those who state that the New Testament makes no reference to premarital sex relations would do well to make a careful study of the New Testament. They may be "outstanding" scholars, but they are certainly "standing outside" of the New Testament on the subject of premarital sex.

DO CHURCHES EQUATE SEX WITH SIN?

In *Parade* magazine, July 30, 1972, Dr. William H. Masters and his wife Virginia Johnson Masters blame the churches for the fact that fifty percent of all marriages in the United States are handicapped by poor sex life, which they say is probably the leading cause of marital discord and divorce. Then they say that "many religions equate sex with sin." Since the Masters were talking about family life in the United States, the word "religions" must mean Protestants, Catholics, and Jews.

Churches seem to be the favorite "whipping boys" for the radical thinkers who promote sexual permissiveness. Another similar example is Hugh Hefner, of *Playboy*, who takes the position that "through the centuries the church has emphasized sex primarily as sin." It is correct to admit that the churches in our society have been slow in developing effective Christian sex education. On the other hand, to say that religious people have always identified sex with sin, and still do today, is utterly false. I have never known an intelligent Protestant, Catholic, or Jew who believed that sex, as such, is sinful. They have always said that, not sex, but the *misuse* and *abuse* of sex is sinful. The philosophy of the Masters and Hefner would probably cause them to reject even the existence of "sin." It is amusing that people with nonreligious ideas speak out with such authority on religious matters.

Let us examine the charge that "Jews and Christians have always thought and still think of sex as sinful." The Hebrew Scriptures state, "So God created man [mankind] in His own image ... male and female created he them. ... and God saw everything that he had made and behold it was *very good*. ... Therefore shall a man leave his father and mother and shall cleave unto his wife: and they shall be one flesh [including the sexual relationship]. And they were both naked, the man and his wife, and were not ashamed" (Genesis 1:27, 31; 2:24, 25, italics mine). In other Old Testament passages sexual intercourse in marriage is described as the normal method for husband and wife to meet their sexual needs, for example, Proverbs 5:15-19 and the Song of Solomon 2:6 and 8:3. Note that these passages do not refer to reproduction. In the New Testament, the Pharisees questioned Jesus about divorce. He repeated words from the book of Genesis (Matthew

19:3-6 and Mark 10:6-9), and reminded the Pharisees that "from the beginning of creation" the sexual one-flesh relationship had been the plan of God for man and woman in marriage. Other New Testament writers followed the same interpretation, as in 1 Corinthians 7:2-5, 1 Thessalonians 4:1-8 (RSV) and Hebrews 13:4. Note again that these passages make no reference to reproduction, which is discussed elsewhere in the Hebrew-Christian Scriptures.

Martin Luther left the monastery, married at age forty-two, and had three children. Luther taught that the body as it was made was something good and that sex life in marriage is fully acceptable to God. He wrote,

> Man is indeed obliged to marry, for the simple reason that God in creation commanded him to do so. God created man with such a strong sex urge that man is left with no choice. His desire for gratification with the opposite sex is as natural as the flame that consumes the straw when it is kindled by fire.[1]

It is true that during biblical times and across the centuries there have been groups of thinkers who have taught that the "flesh is evil" and the "spirit is good," but they were neither Hebrew nor Christian. (They were followers of Greek dualism and Persian Manichaeism.) It is true that some of these false ideas crept into the early churches and caused many problems on through the Middle Ages. When church leaders like Augustine (A.D. 354-430) and Thomas Aquinas (1225-1274) thought that man was better off if he could get along without sex, they were reflecting Greek and Persian ideas and not Hebrew-Christian thought. To hold modern Christianity responsible for the non-Christian ideas of Augustine and Aquinas is like holding the American Medical Association responsible for some of the ridiculous medical practices of one thousand years ago.

During the last fifty years hundreds of Christian scholars have stated thousands of times, through the spoken and written word, that sex, as such, is not evil, but that the

[1] Oscar E. Feucht, ed., Sex and the Church (St. Louis: Concordia Publishing House, 1961), pp. 77, 78.

Creator-God created sex for marriage as a positive good.

In the light of an honest interpretation of the historical facts, it is impossible to understand how educated people like the Masters, who ought to know better, can continue to parrot the falsehood that religions (Protestants, Catholics, and Jews) glorify sexual abstinence and equate sex with sin. I would like to invite them and their tribe to move into the twentieth century.

IS SEX NATURAL—LIKE BREATHING, EATING, AND SLEEPING?

The July 30, 1972 issue of Parade magazine quoted William Masters and Virginia Johnson Masters (the St. Louis sex-research team) as saying, "Sex is a natural function like breathing, eating, and sleeping." Without clear thinking, many people buy this idea and ask, "Since this is true, why does society make such a fuss about sex—that which is normal and natural?"

I cannot buy this idea as enthusiastically as some do because it is only a part truth. This theory is saying, "Is not sex as natural as hunger for food and thirst for water?" Often the advocates of sexual permissiveness quickly answer this question with a "yes" and defend the idea vigorously. This "nature" idea is especially appealing to youth. In fact, it appeals to all of us. And there is some solid truth here. Sex is natural! It is as normal a part of creation as breathing, eating, and sleeping. However, the permissive thinkers fail to point out that there are some major differences between human sex life and the other natural bodily functions.

Dr. Sylvanus M. Duvall has pointed out three major reasons why sex hunger is different from other human hungers, such as hunger for food and thirst for drink. We summarize his three points as follows:

1. The denial of sexual satisfaction in life produces little or no harmful physical effects. Those people who do not eat food and drink water (and sleep) will soon weaken

physically and die, and we will have a funeral. For a man or woman to go through life without having sexual intercourse produces no comparable physical harm.

2. The satisfaction of hunger for food and thirst for water need not have any harmful social or moral effects on a person. Selection and eating of food and drink can be largely a private matter and has no social significance for society as a whole. On the other hand, satisfying the sex hunger through sexual permissiveness has major social consequences. There is the possibility of pregnancy and venereal disease. Society is rightly concerned about both of these, and must, therefore, have some moral codes. Even if we have the know-how to control birth, we still need moral codes because of the human factor involved. Those who assume the least responsibility for having children also assume the least responsibility for properly developing them, and thus society must toe the line and take care of them.

3. Satisfying the sex hunger in sexual permissiveness involves another person or persons. The food and drink that a man consumes may be prepared by someone else and brought to him by a waitress. Such services rarely result in any serious personal involvement. These services are in an entirely different category from the satisfaction of sexual hunger derived directly from the body of another person.

Therefore, when all the truth is considered, Dr. Duvall concludes, and I agree with him, that the idea that sex hunger is "like any other hunger is nonsense."[2] In courtship, marriage, and the family, as well as in total life, we must be careful about majoring on small part-truths!

WHAT ARE THE SOCIAL OBJECTIONS TO PREMARITAL SEX?

1. Society objects to premarital sex because of the

[2] Sylvanus M. Duvall, *Men, Women, and Morals* (New York: Association Press, 1952), pp. 37, 38.

ever-present danger of pregnancy. During 1973 there were over 300,000 known cases of babies born out of wedlock in the United States. This figure does not include fourteen states that keep little or no records. Over 300,000! And just one is *one too many,* especially if the mother is your daughter or your sister. Whenever there is a premarriage pregnancy, serious decisions must be made quickly, and there is no "happy" solution possible. It is a tragedy for all concerned. In the light of the "300,000," (and that number is still increasing), it is very difficult to understand the logic of some radicals who keep repeating the idea that there is now no danger of premarriage pregnancy.

2. Society objects to premarital sex because sexual promiscuity promotes venereal disease. Dr. Evelyn Duvall in her lovely little book *Why Wait Till Marriage?* states that in 1947 there were 107,716 cases of syphilis in the United States. (When penicillin was first discovered, the sex-permissive advocates laughed with glee and said that now the narrow-minded moralists can't use V.D. as an objection to premarital sex.) By 1953 there were only 9,551 cases reported. Here was progress. We were all thankful. But by 1958 the downward trend reversed itself, and Dr. Duvall reports that "by 1963 after five years of annual increases, there were four and one-half times as many cases as were reported in 1957—an increase of 448 percent!" She reports that "gonorrhea is even more widespread and prevalent than syphilis."[3] Since then, this high rate of both of these diseases has continued. For example, in June 1970, the number of cases of syphilis was 27.3 percent higher than in June 1969. Today the Medical Health Association is calling V.D. the worst disease epidemic in our society. How can the sex radicals still say that V.D. cannot be used as a valid objection to sexual promiscuity? V.D. follows sexual promiscuity as the night follows the day. And the saddest part of it all is that as

---

[3] Evelyn Millis Duvall, *Why Wait Till Marriage?* (New York: Association Press, 1965), pp. 54, 55.

the epidemic continues, the age of the boys and girls who get caught in the trap is becoming lower and lower. It is a distressing and depressing comment on our social order.

3. In courtship, premarital sex promotes guilt feelings that often destroy the relationship. Soon couples begin to find fault with each other. They begin to blame each other. Often they come to hate each other. Dr. and Mrs. Judson Landis quote a boy as saying, "Once we began to have sex relations, I lost all interest in getting married." This is often par for the course. Premarital sex is divisive! It promotes distrust, fear, and suspicion, whereas sexual self-control until marriage develops confidence, faith, and trust—those attitudes necessary for marriage growth, maturity, and happiness.

4. Norman Vincent Peale has been a well-known New York pastor and marriage counselor for many years. Having counseled hundreds of couples, he has concluded that premarital sexual promiscuity does not work, but that waiting until marriage brings a depth and intensity to sex life in marriage that can be found in no other way.[4]

5. Premarital sex takes the edge off the honeymoon. The modern honeymoon is an excellent American social institution. As life moves on, the memories of a happy honeymoon will linger among the choicest memories of a couple's courtship and marriage. One study indicates that 87 percent of couples who practiced self-control until marriage had a honeymoon, as compared to only 47 percent of couples who had been sexually intimate before marriage.[5] The reason for the sharp decline is obvious. Premarital sex takes the edge off the honeymoon. It destroys the meaning and the value of the honeymoon.

6. Robert O. Blood says that waiting until marriage has a long-range advantage in that "it provides a secure set-

---

[4] Norman Vincent Peale, *Sin, Sex, and Self-Control* (Garden City, New York: Doubleday, 1965), pp. 90, 91.
[5] Eugene J. Kanin and David H. Howard, *American Sociological Review*, 23:5, 558.

ting for children conceived from sexual intercourse."[6] There is a long period from birth to adult maturity. The basic needs of growing children are not sexual but emotional. The bent of a child's personality development is determined by the overall parent-child relationships. The only adequate environment for growing children is a home where a happy husband and wife are deeply in love with each other and are deeply committed to each other. Sexual self-control before marriage promotes this type of family life environment in marriage. Christian leaders have not capitalized on the fact that the humanistic and materialistic theories about premarital (and extramarital) sex does not provide adequate environment for growing children.

7. Also, Blood thinks that drawing a distinction between singleness and marriage "accentuates the importance of marriage and contributes to its stability."[7] It is important that people in society know who is married to whom and have a record of each marriage. Under a system of pre-marriage (and marriage) promiscuity, the line between singleness and marriage becomes blurred until there is utter social and legal chaos. The Hebrew-Christian system that calls for sexual control before marriage draws a line between singleness and marriage that emphasizes the importance of marriage and contributes to its stability. History points to the significant fact that enduring responsible family life is the cornerstone of civilization.

8. Finally, there are very few people, if any, in society who really believe in promiscuous premarital sex. It is logically impossible for a mature, intelligent person to do so. Some do say that they believe in premarital sex and defend it, but their belief is often very foggy, inconsistent, and contradictory. It amounts to "I believe in it for me." To believe logically in premarital sexual intercourse, a man must defend the right of his mother to have had sex relations with any man before she was married. He must

---

[6] Robert O. Blood, *Marriage*, 2nd ed. (New York: The Free Press, 1969), p. 157.

[7] Ibid.

defend the right of his sister to have sex relations with any man before she is married. He must defend the right of his wife, his daughter, his daughter-in-law, and his granddaughter to have sex relations with any man before they are married. Few civilized persons could really believe and accept this. It is intelligent and logical for a man to treat other women as he would have other men treat his mother, sister, wife, daughter, daughter-in-law, and granddaughter.

WHAT ARE SOME OF THE ARGUMENTS USED IN FAVOR OF PREMARITAL SEX?

Much of the public writings on sex flowing from the propaganda media and from certain social scientists seems planned to refute arguments in favor of waiting until marriage. A person who waits is pictured as being old-fashioned, back-woodsy, and unscientifc. On the other hand, arguments in favor of premarital sex are presented as being natural, moral, social, and scientific. Many fine young people are at a loss to know how to meet this permissive propaganda. Let us examine five of the main arguments used to advocate premarital sex.

1. "It gives relief from biological tension." This argument assumes that sex is biological and ignores the spiritual, the psychological, the emotional, the moral, and the social aspects of sex. It ignores the fact that girls have little or no trouble controlling their sex drive. Premarital sex forces girls into the picture and this reduces a girl to a thing to be used to physically satisfy selfish boys. It violates her rights as a person. The argument ignores the fact that the Creator who gave young men a strong sex drive also gave them a means of controlling it until marriage—nocturnal seminal emissions.[8] In order to "make

---

[8] See chapter 9, "A Program of Sexual Control for Young Men: A Study of Masturbation," Herbert J. Miles, *Sexual Understanding Before Marriage* (Grand Rapids: Zondervan Publishing House, 1971), pp. 137-162.

a buck" the propaganda media imply that the male biological need for sexual release is really much stronger than it is. When a boy becomes preoccupied with sex, it tends to become a major problem. Most scholars agree that sexual permissiveness is often psychological and cultural, rather than physical.

2. "The failure of couples to have premarital sex is the cause of courtship quarreling." Those who advance this argument have no scientific evidence to back it up. What are the real causes for courtship quarreling? They are generally selfishness, insecurity, jealousy, opposite life interests, the approach of a third party, personality conflicts, laziness, dates without plans, boredom, etc.

3. "Premarital sex is a good test for sexual compatibility and is good preparation for effective sex life in marriage." This argument is without scientific foundation. Dr. Paul Popenoe studied the sex life of 2,000 married women. Eighty-six percent of those who were virgins at marriage had achieved sexual adjustment (orgasm) at the time the research was made, as compared to eighty-five percent of the nonvirgins. My own research on the sex life of 151 married couples published in my book *Sexual Happiness in Marriage* (Zondervan, 1967) refutes the idea that premarriage sex is necessary for sexual happiness in marriage. Couples who wait until marriage have more *stable* and *successful* marriages and have just as much sexual efficiency. The idea that couples must have premarriage sex experience to have sexual happiness in marriage is a phony argument. When couples are not married, they are not married! It is impossible to test marriage in the state of singleness. Sex is not something that can be "tested" by some "fly-by-night" experience as you use a thermometer to test temperature. Sexual adjustment in marriage is something that has to be learned in the privacy of married love, trust, tenderness, and understanding. Often it takes many weeks or months to achieve good adjustment.

4. "Would you buy a pair of shoes without trying them on?" Dr. Henry A. Bowman says we should

answer such questions in the negative but add there is a difference between a girl and a pair of shoes. What happens to a pair of shoes is inconsequential. What happens to a girl is of great consequence.... One does not consider establishing a life-long relationship with a pair of shoes. There is no chance that by accident a pair of shoes will have little ones. So the comparison breaks down and becomes meaningless.[9]

5. "Many brides who enter marriage as virgins are afraid of sex; premarriage experience will give them confidence." Often it is the very premarriage experience (that failed as far as they are concerned) that makes them afraid of sex in marriage. Honest now! Girls are not afraid of sex! They *are* afraid of premarriage pregnancy! They are afraid of immorality! They are afraid of ruining their marriage! All society has to do is give girls the right values, good attitudes, and a normal sex education from childhood until marriage, including thorough premarriage counseling, and they will enter marriage with as much confidence and assurance as boys.

Thus it behooves young people to stay with their conviction that sex belongs to marriage. Dr. and Mrs. Judson Landis state that "normally well adjusted young people will suffer no ill effects from following a plan which includes self-control and emphasizes avoidance of excessive sex interest until they can marry. The advantages are all on the side of this course of action."[10]

WHAT ABOUT SEX DURING ENGAGEMENT?

Many fine young people object to unbridled sexual permissiveness. Yet they feel that during engagement sexual intercourse is in order. They reason that "during engagement a couple is in love; the wedding date is set. They are going to be married." Then they ask, "What is

[9] Henry A. Bowman, *Marriage for Moderns*, 6th ed. (New York: McGraw-Hill, Inc., 1970) p. 140.
[10] Landis and Landis, *Building a Successful Marriage*, 3rd ed. (New York: Prentice-Hall, 1958), p. 231.

the difference between an engaged couple three months or three weeks before marriage and the same couple after marriage? Is there really any difference?"

Yes, there are some differences—some major, significant differences.

1. Before marriage a couple is involved in and dependent on two separate economic systems. The boy and girl are each a part of their respective family units. Their parents are responsible to them for food, clothing, shelter, and protection. After marriage, however, the couple is a separate economic unit, and the two together are now responsible for their own food, clothing, shelter, protection, and other needs.

2. Before marriage the boy and girl have been conditioned by approximately two decades of psychological, emotional, social, and spiritual experience with their own families. Most of their teachings, beliefs, values, and ways of life have now become a real part of their inner self. Of course, after marriage they still will love their parents and cherish the values and relationships received from them; but then they must depend upon each other for inner strength, stability, and support.

3. Before marriage both the boy and the girl are identified legally with their own individual parents. They are two separate legal entities and each is free to act within the framework of his or her own family according to the laws of his or her particular state. After marriage, these two legal entities are merged into one unit. They are legally bound to each other and are legally responsible to each other. Although they are still the son and daughter of their own parents, their legal status has been changed to that of a family unit.

4. Before marriage they are not one in the eyes of the social community. Their relatives, friends, and community associates see them as members of their own families and expect them to perform the social and moral roles of single people. After marriage their relatives and

friends see them as members of a new family unit and expect them to perform the social and moral roles of married people.

5. Before marriage, if a pregnancy should occur, there is immediately before them a mountain of personal, emotional, social, and spiritual problems that would tend to be a major burden to them the rest of their lives. After marriage, if and when a pregnancy occurs, the baby would be accepted, loved, and cared for as an equal member of the new family unit and of the community.

Furthermore, the argument favoring sex during engagement tends to ignore two important facts: (1) From one-third to one-half of all engagements are broken and (2) a social sanction of sexual intercourse during engagement would tend to encourage large numbers of phony engagements for sex purposes.

SHOULD A SINGLE GIRL TAKE THE "PILL" TO AVOID PREGNANCY?

In recent years medical science has developed an oral contraceptive—a small pill that can be taken by mouth that will prevent pregnancy. The pill is a mixture of hormones. Different drug companies use slightly different formulas. For example, one formula calls for a wife to start taking the pill five days after the beginning of her ovulation period. She is instructed by her doctor to take one every day for a given period, which is determined by the length of her menstrual cycle. It may vary from sixteen to twenty days. The pills thus taken stop the ovulation period (the sending out of an ovum from the ovary). Since there is no ovum sent out, there can be no pregnancy. After the sixteenth day, the wife ceases to take the pill in order to allow the regular menstrual period to occur. Then five days after the beginning of each menstrual period, she starts to take the pills again, and this process is repeated month after month. These pills at present are the most effective contraceptive. When taken carefully according to a physician's instructions, they are almost 100 percent effective.[11]

The question before us is this: Is it within the scope of Christian morals for single girls to take the pill in order to avoid pregnancy from premarital sex relations? The following letter from a prominent clergyman illustrates the problem.

> Recently a mother, Mrs. X, came to me, her pastor, with the following problem. She said, "Pastor, my daughter is, I believe, a good girl. We have tried to give her religious training. But we cannot be with her all the time, and are aware that, as any young person, she is under influences other than the home and the church that make severe demands upon her. Recently I have been wondering if I should introduce my daughter to 'the Pill'; I hope she will not engage in premarital sex, but just in case, would not a controlled situation be better than an unwanted pregnancy? Now Pastor, I know what the Bible says about sex. But I also know I must relate to my daughter in today's world. What should I and what can I do?" What can the mother do? And how can a pastor help both the mother and the daughter?

This question is complex and involved. Yet it is crucial to many mothers and daughters in our day, thanks to the immoral cultural drift promoted by vested interests, social climbers, and the philosophy of materialistic humanism. Many parents have a feeling of helplessness. The time for this drift to be met head-on by moral and religious forces is long overdue. We must stop ducking this question. Today's world, as bad as it is, is not as bad as the world in which Christianity was born. In that world woman was something to be used and sex was something to be associated with religious worship. Yet today the birth of babies out of wedlock is one of the most sad and destructive social burdens in our society. God forbid that any clergyman, or any Christian mother should encourage it in any form.

---

[11] For further discussion, see my book *Sexual Happiness in Marriage* (Grand Rapids: Zondervan Publishing House, 1967), pp. 106, 107.

Let us examine the question "What can and should Mrs. X do?" She needs to think very carefully through the temptation to give her single daughter the pill to avoid a pregnancy. Some observations are in order.

1. The question seems to assume that her daughter (let's call her Jane) must either use the pill or have an unwanted pregnancy. Is there not a third alternative, namely morality and sexual self-control until marriage?

2. If Mrs. X introduces Jane to the pill, what is she saying about her daughter's moral stability? Assuming Jane is, as she says, "a good girl" with "religious training," what will she think about the way her own mother trusts her?

3. Mrs. X says she "knows what the Bible says about sex." As a Christian, why doesn't she take the Bible more seriously? In the Bible, the word "fornication" means sex relations by a person who has never been married. "Adultery" means sex relations of a married person with someone other than his or her married companion. In several biblical lists of evils, both fornication and adultery are given and are made to be equal with each other. Also, fornication is said to be equal with drunkenness, stealing, murder, and idolatry. The Bible says that people guilty of these actions (1) are not led by the Spirit of God, (2) are directed by motives that come out of evil hearts, (3) are spiritually unclean because of these actions, and (4) cannot inherit the kingdom of God. Fornication with or without the pill is not a Christian option.

4. If Mrs. X introduces Jane to the pill, is she not encouraging her to be immoral? If Jane should be guilty of premarital sex, hiding behind the protection of the pill, does this not make Mrs. X share in the responsibility for her immoral actions?

5. When word gets out that Jane is on the pill, and it will, can we not expect Jane to be less resistant to young men's advances? Is not giving Jane insurance against pregnancy equal to inviting a test? Is this the way for a mother to build strength of character in the life of her daughter?

6. Mrs. X seems to be placing second things first. Is she

not more concerned about what society thinks about a premarital pregnancy than what God thinks about immoral behavior? Is she not more interested in self and present expediency than in what is right or what is long-range social and moral progress? Has she not allowed her personal fears to overcome her rationality?

7. When Mrs. X says, "I must relate my daughter to this present world," what does she mean? Is she not saying that our culture approves and practices premarital sex? Therefore, Christians should bend with the times and follow the immoral way of culture? I cannot buy this reasoning. It is humanistic relativism; that is, it is right for the individual to follow what everybody else is doing. The truth is that not every youth is guilty of practicing premarital sex, and it is not right for those who do.

Mrs. X must understand that I am not arguing against the use of contraceptives, nor am I trying to promote the birth of babies out of wedlock. And yes, it is difficult to draw a line between the social problems involved in babies being born out of wedlock and premarital sex. Both present major social problems. However, it is immorality that causes babies to be born out of wedlock and not vice versa. Babies born out of wedlock are the result and not the cause. Why don't we change the cause rather than promote sinful and unsocial results? To get rid of moral and spiritual standards will erode and destroy our organized family life upon which effective society and civilization rests.

WHAT CAUSES MALE SEXUAL IMPOTENCE?

I received the following pertinent letter from Robert G. Wells, M.D., Chief of the Department of Obstetrics and Gynecology, Long Beach Memorial Hospital, Long Beach, California.

> **I have been extremely impressed with your excellent book,** Sexual Happiness in Marriage. **I have used this book in counseling and lecturing, and have found it to be the**

very best discussion on the role of sex in today's marriages that I have ever read. One question that continues to come up at the time of my talks to various groups of young people is "male impotence." This is an exceedingly difficult area for physicians to counsel in, and I would greatly appreciate your comments that I could use to deal with this problem.

It is refreshing to know that a busy physician takes time to counsel and lecture young people on personal problems related to courtship and marriage. May his tribe increase.

Impotence is the inability of a man to experience sexual intercourse with a woman. This is one of those delicate subjects that has been "swept under the rug" far too long. It is a frank question, and it deserves a frank, dignified answer. In almost all cases the cause of male sexual impotence is not biological, but rather it is mental and emotional.

1. Sometimes single young men masturbate excessively until they are sexually exhausted and temporarily cannot operate sexually.[12]

2. During courtship, frequent sessions involving long sexual arousal without release may cause temporary male impotence.

3. A few frightened bridegrooms who have worried about their virility since puberty may experience temporary impotence on the wedding night.

4. A young married man in the first months of his marriage may have sex relations excessively until he is exhausted sexually and may have temporary impotence. He just needs to slow down.

5. When young married couples have an extreme lack of privacy for intimate relationships, temporary impotence may result.

6. Concern and fear over the possibility of premature ejaculation may cause temporary impotence.

7. The long practice in marriage of withdrawal before

---

[12] For a detailed discussion of masturbation, see my book *Sexual Understanding Before Marriage* (Grand Rapids: Zondervan Publishing House, 1971), chapter 9.

ejaculation, as a routine contraceptive practice, may cause impotence.

8. A strong sense of guilt about secret sex affairs, past or present, may cause a husband to experience some impotence.

9. Excessive anger, hostility, excitement, fear, and worry may be a cause.

10. It is possible that long and excessive concentration and hard work over the years at one's occupation may cause some impotence.

11. A man who tends to hate women in general and is hostile to his wife may experience impotence.

12. An excessively selfish egocentric man who loves himself and no one else may encounter the problem of impotence.

13. In later years, a man's fear of declining virility and excessive efforts to prove himself often cause the problem of impotence.

14. Research indicates, as physicians know, that excessive smoking, the drinking of alcohol, and the use of tranquilizers, sedatives, and narcotics may reduce potency.

I suppose we could sum up these fourteen ideas by saying that male impotence is caused by fear, sexual excesses, lack of normal sex education, a twisted set of values, and immature and insecure personalities.

Treatment would include a thorough, positive sex education, a healthy attitude toward sex, women, marriage, and the worth of human personality, a healthy self-consistent set of values based on Judeo-Christian assumptions, a balanced, mature personality, and avoidance of sexual excesses. In extreme psychological cases, psychiatric help is needed.

WHAT ARE THE FACTS ABOUT KINSEY'S STUDY OF FEMALE SEX LIFE?

The late Dr. Alfred Kinsey's study[13] is often quoted as

---

[13] Alfred Kinsey, *Sexual Behavior in the Human Female* (Philadelphia: William B. Saunders Company, 1953).

the authority in defense of current looseness in sexual standards. What are the facts about Kinsey's study?

To discuss Kinsey's studies now, twenty years after they were published, is like beating a dead horse. And yet, because of a few radical thinkers who still swear by Kinsey's studies as the "Bible on Sex," it is in order to discuss this question.

I approve of responsible social scientists making scientific studies to establish truth about human sexual behavior. I personally spent six years studying the sexual pattern of behavior of 151 married couples.[14] Such research helps us to understand the relationship of normal sex life in marriage to health, personality development, and family happiness. It helps to understand the relationship of abnormal sex life to disease, delinquency, mental and emotional disturbances, vice, and crime. Kinsey had a moral and social right to make a study of sex. Why then has there been so much criticism of his study? Let us look at the facts.

Dr. Alfred Kinsey, professor of zoology (he specialized in studying wasps) at the University of Indiana, made the studies, assisted by several others, including Dr. Wardell Pomeroy. The study was made in and around the University of Indiana and the University of Chicago. The researchers asked women to volunteer to be interviewed in detail about their sex life. They interviewed 5,940 women. Over 300 questions were asked, and each interview took about two and one-half hours. The following facts are stated in the book about the research sample: Those women of the sample who were married averaged age 27 at their first marriage.[15] This is greatly out of line, since the average age at first marriage for girls in 1950 was about 20.5 years. Almost one-third of the married women were either separated or divorced.[16] Fifteen percent of the sample had

---

[14] See my book *Sexual Happiness in Marriage* (Grand Rapids: Zondervan Publishing House, 1967), pp. 129-146.

[15] Kinsey, *Sexual Behavior*, p. 426.

[16] Ibid., p. 32.

two or more premarriage pregnancies.[17] Of the total number in the sample, 2,094 women stated they had experienced premarital sexual intercourse. Each woman was asked to estimate the number of times she had had such relations. When added, it totaled approximately 460,000 times. A little arithmetic indicates that the 2,094 women of the sample had had premarriage sexual intercourse an average of 220 times each. About one-half of them had had such relations with from two to over twenty different partners.[18] In the past we have had names for women like this—harlots, prostitutes.

What kind of women would volunteer to talk to a strange man about her sex life? Dr. Judson Landis was right when he said that these women were not representative of American women either in college or out. Thus a major criticism of Kinsey's study is that the sample was not representative. It was very distorted and unscientific.

A second major criticism concerns the biased interpretation Kinsey and many admiring scholars gave to his studies. In spite of the fact that Kinsey tried to be objective about his approach, his interpretation promoted the philosophy of sexual permissiveness. He overemphasized the biological side of sex and all but ignored the social, moral, mental, emotional, and spiritual aspects. Imagine writing a book on sex and ignoring such things as love, fidelity, self-control, self-realization, and social responsibility! Dr. Karl Menninger, who admired Kinsey's mathematical accuracy, challenged the value of the study. He said, "Kinsey's compulsion to force human sexual behavior into a zoological frame of reference leads him to repudiate or neglect human psychology, and to see normality as that which is natural in the sense that it is what is practiced by animals."[19] This book is an insult to American women.

During the last twenty years, there have been many other studies concerning sexual behavior (including Landis, Er-

---

[17] Ibid., p. 327.
[18] Ibid., pp. 327, 336.
[19] *Saturday Review*, September 26, 1953, 36:30.

hanann, Christiansen, Kirkendall, and, yes, Masters **and** Johnson) that are superior to Kinsey's work. Any professor or book today that quotes Kinsey as sexual "holy writ" is like one who drives a Model T Ford at the corner of Main and Broadway.

Dr. Evelyn Mills Duvall said, "Re-analysis of the Kinsey studies fails to substantiate the claim that the premaritally experienced make better marriage adjustment over the years. Far more research than is now available is needed to find reliable bases for this or other 'arguments' for premarital sex relations."[20]

The Kinsey worshipers are guilty of willfully promoting one of the most deadly doctrines of all history, namely, "Everybody is doing it; therefore, it is right."[21]

---

[20] Evelyn Millis Duvall, *The Art of Dating* (New York: Association Press, 1968), p. 203.

[21] One of the major problems blocking intelligent courtship and preparation for marriage is that young people have not received the necessary facts and materials to challenge permissive arguments on the spot and expose them by pointing out the false assumptions upon which they are based. My book, *Sexual Understanding Before Marriage* (Grand Rapids: Zondervan Publishing House, 1971) is designed to (1) help young people convincingly reject and refute the sexual permissive arguments and (2) help them properly relate sex to their courtship and marriage by controlling and directing it into divinely planned channels of expression.

9

Planning the Wedding Ceremony

WHAT ABOUT A SECRET MARRIAGE?

There have been thousands of engaged young couples who have toyed with the idea of a secret marriage. The following letter is a typical example.

> We are engaged to be married, but our parents want us to wait for one year before marriage. We are both nineteen. Both sets of parents feel that we ought to be at least twenty before we are married. When two people love each other as dearly as we do, it is very difficult to wait a year for marriage. Recently we have been discussing the idea of getting married secretly and keeping it a secret for several months. We are intrigued with the idea, but have decided to write and ask for your opinion. After all, we love each other, we are engaged, and we are going to get married. Why not get married secretly? We think it would be fun.
>
> Doyle and Jill

The sacred, social, and sexual nature of love and marriage leads me to the following observations about secret marriages:

1. A secret marriage is a violation of one of the Ten Commandments, for it is living a lie. We have been taught since childhood—by parents, by the church, by the school, and by society—that it is wrong to tell a lie. Yet a secret marriage is living a public lie about a major and certainly a sacred relationship in life. Furthermore, it is impossible to keep a secret marriage secret very long. A couple must face reality sooner or later, and it is much easier to face

it at the time of marriage than to have to face it later, after living a lie for some weeks or months.

2. A secret marriage is a violation of the sacred obligations that we have to our parents, our relatives, our friends, and our community. Our parents, relatives, friends, and community have meant much in our lives, helping us in thousands of ways. They have made possible our growing to maturity and adulthood. It seems to me that they have a right to know about our courtship. They have at least some right to help us plan it, and certainly they have a right to rejoice with us at the time of our wedding ceremony. Thus a secret marriage violates our parents, our relatives, friends, the total community—the very people that we ought to love and appreciate most.

3. A secret marriage will cause a person regret in the future. As one looks back on a secret marriage, the day will come when he will be sorry. He will admit it to himself, even though he does not admit it publicly, and will say within himself, "If I had it to do over again, I would do it right."

4. Finally, I suspect a secret marriage for what it really is in many cases. I suspect that the couple is simply anxious to have sex relations, and the secret marriage makes it possible for them to have sex relations within the law, within conscience, and without having guilt feelings.

A married couple must live in society. No couple should move into any type of marriage that is not approved by the society in which they live. It is socially necessary for any society to know who is married to whom.

Parents, relatives, friends, and your community have a right to know about your wedding and rejoice with you as it takes place.

WHAT IS THE FINANCIAL COST OF FORMAL CHURCH WEDDINGS?

The commercial world and social climbers have led us to make complete fools of ourselves in our society in relationship to occasions that should be very personal and sacred in life's journey. These occasions include Christmas, Easter, Thanksgiving, the 4th of July, birthdays, funerals and, yes, weddings. The emphasis in modern formal church weddings is on things, color, costumes, decorations, food, empty formality, complexity, materialistic concepts, and a "keep-up-with-the-Joneses" kind of sophistication. In some extremely formal and expensive weddings, the focus on such trifles loses sight of the wonderful girl and boy that are being married. The meaning and purpose of the occasion are easily lost in the shuffle.

A study of seventy formal church weddings was made in 1959 and again thirteen years later, in 1972, involving one hundred sixty-two weddings. A formal church wedding was defined as "a public wedding, held in a church, that was characterized by formal invitations, dress, decorations, ceremony and reception." These two studies involved the weddings of friends and relatives of church-related college students in the southeastern part of the United States. The questionnaire was used to measure the cost of weddings, including paid help, flowers, decorations, dress, the reception, license, blood-test fee, invitations and postage, photographer and pictures, the cost of the newspaper story, the rings, bridesmaids' luncheon, the rehearsal dinner, gifts for members of the wedding party, gifts between bride and groom, thank-you notes and postage, and other items. The study did not include the cost of the honeymoon. In 1959, the average cost of the seventy wedding ceremonies was $1,311.37. Note that most couples cut costs where possible. If a 1959 couple had paid for the total cost of the wedding at the same price each item cost (for those who used it), the wedding would have cost $1,804.66. In other words, by omitting some items, the seventy couples saved on the average of nearly $500.00 per wedding. Since it is difficult to measure all of the actual costs, it was concluded that a total formal church wedding in 1959 would have cost over $2,000.00.

But financial inflation and an increase of wedding formality increased wedding costs by 1972. In the 1972 repeat study of 162 formal church weddings, the couples paid an average of $1,726.61 per wedding. If a 1972 couple had paid for the total cost of the wedding at the same price each item cost (for those who used it) the wedding would have cost $2,137.16. In other words, the 1972 couples cut cost on the average of over $400.00 per wedding. If all of the actual costs had been measured, I would conclude that a total 1972 formal wedding would have cost $2,500.00 or more.

In the 162 weddings in the 1972 study, the average cost per item was as follows:

> minister, $19.76; organist, $14.57; soloist, $12.60; wedding consultant, $41.13; other paid help, $25.79; all flowers, $115.68; church decorations, $94.45; bride's wedding dress, $139.91; wedding veil, $35.47; trousseau, $125.17; dress for members of family, $125.09; other dress expense, $91.89 (unfortunately the questionnaire did not list the cost of the groom's attire); total cost of reception, $299.33; license, $6.72; invitations and postage, $83.13; photographer and pictures, $106.75; gifts for members of the wedding party, $53.67; thank-you notes and postage, $32.16; newspaper expense, $15.43; rehearsal dinner, $104.14; rings—engagement and both wedding bands—$329.99; bridesmaid's luncheon, $45.65; gifts between bride and groom, $68.66; blood test fee, $9.25; and other items, $146.83.

WHEW! Talk about affluence! And these were largely Southern middle-class weddings. Yet these figures are small change when compared to the cost of some upper-middle- and upper-class weddings in our society. Some large city hotel receptions alone cost $10,000.00. If we may judge the future by the past, we may expect continued increase in wedding costs.

This is rather expensive formality. Some extremely expensive wedding ceremonies tend to exalt external formality above internal purpose. They seem to substitute empty symbols for external realities. The extreme cost of some formal weddings causes me to ask, "Is it wise for young people to follow blindly drifting, derelict culture?"

Is it not a genuine case of the tail (empty formality) wagging the dog (personal freedom) to do so? I do not mean to criticize formal church weddings, as such. I recommend that the couple plan a formal church wedding and invite the public through the local newspaper and the church bulletin. I do not want to criticize merchants who sell flowers and the wedding attire that is ordered for a wedding. I *do* want to criticize those in our society whose first and only commandment seems to be "Thou shalt keep up with, and get ahead of, the Joneses."

WHAT ARE SOME WAYS TO CUT THE COST OF FORMAL CHURCH WEDDINGS?

It is acceptable for any couple to decide to have a small home wedding. They are beautiful, impressive, and sacred —and they are less expensive than the formal church wedding. Yet, *I recommend a formal church wedding* in which the public is invited through the newspaper and the church bulletin, because a couple owes so much to so many relatives, friends, and the total community. To invite the public amounts to saying to everyone, "Thank you for the wonderful part you have played in our lives, all of which makes this wonderful day (our marriage) possible."

In order to cut the cost of a formal church wedding, a couple should plan the wedding on the same financial plane that they plan to live on and the level they can afford. A lot of wedding expense is due to blind routine tradition rather than necessity. Use originality and creative ingenuity. Do not be afraid to be different so long as it is in the limits of dignity and good taste. It is wise to shop around for the best prices. Plan a budget for your wedding, and let it guide you. A budget tells your money where to go and does not leave you wondering, afterwards, where it went. A couple should do their own planning instead of turning it over to their family, friends, or a department-store consultant. Ask for and listen to advice and suggestions, but make your own decisions. It is easy to resolve that you are going to have a simple, inexpensive wedding, but let me warn readers that social pressures will be so great that it will take a determined, iron will to resist spending more than you need to spend.

There are many ways a couple may cut the cost of their wedding ceremony and not destroy the social dignity and the spiritual significance of the occasion. Some couples are able to use a minister, an organist, or soloist who are members of the immediate family and who would not accept a fee for being so honored. Use flowers that are in season. Some use flowers and greenery from the woods or from the gardens of close friends or relatives. Arrange the floral decorations yourself and do not use too many flowers. One flower in the hand or pinned on those in the official wedding party speaks volumes.

The bride may make her own wedding dress and veil. Some brides borrow a formal dress from a relative or friend. Some couples rent the wedding dress and tuxedo. Some couples purchase a nice, street-length dress for the bride and a good suit for the groom and wear them many times after the wedding. Each time they wear them it could be symbolic of the day they stood at the wedding altar. Some have only one attendant each at the ceremony. Other couples simply request attendants to wear clothing they already have.

Write out personal notes of invitation. Friends will appreciate the personal touch, and you will save engraving costs. Some send no invitations but invite the public through the newspaper and church bulletin.

You may decide to have the wedding service as a part of a regular worship service. Many churches and pastors would welcome this from members. Most pastors would plan a short sermon on the marriage relationship and the service would not need to be unduly long. Very little in the way of extra flowers or special clothes would be required.

Concerning the wedding reception after the ceremony, have a simple informal reception at the church or at your home. Do not employ a caterer. Make your own small, simple wedding cake. Large, expensive wedding cakes often go to waste. Some couples do not have a formal reception. After the wedding ceremony the official wedding party forms a line in the church foyer and the guests greet and congratulate the couple as they leave the church. During this time, friends and relatives can be introduced. This informal reception saves time for everyone and approximately $300.

There are still other ways to trim the wedding cost. Eliminate the exchange of gifts between bride and groom. Use thank-you notes instead of giving expensive gifts to the wedding party. In some counties free blood tests may be had at the health clinic. (However, certainly the bride should go to a doctor for a premarriage physical examination.) A wedding held in the morning or afternoon is usually less formal and expensive than one held in the evening. Some couples have used impressive recorded music. Others omit the expensive prewedding dinners such as the bridesmaids' luncheon, the bachelor dinner, and the rehearsal dinner.

I do not want readers to think I am a skinflint, a scrooge. I recommend that couples spend some money for rings and some good pictures. Rings and pictures can be permanent and carry endearing symbolic meaning through the years.

The amount of formality and expense of a wedding ceremony has little or nothing to do with the success of the marriage. Most middle-class couples could by careful planning have an impressive formal church wedding ceremony for less than $1,000, thus saving approximately $1,500. It does not cost to march, to carry a Bible, to repeat formal vows, to kneel, or to pray. One father and mother told their daughter that if she would hold her wedding cost under $1,000, they would give her and her husband a check for $1,500 as a wedding gift. Now what could a couple, after marriage, do with $1,500? Maybe a year's further education, an M.A. degree, some furniture, a down

payment on a lot to build on, or a savings account. There
is something that my generation has failed to tell modern
young people. And I can't hold it a secret any long. Here
it is: *It is not a sin to save money!*

SHOULD THE WEDDING CEREMONY BE BUILT AROUND THE BRIDE?

Recently I received the following letter concerned about
formal wedding ceremonies that neglect the groom:

> **Paul and I are planning our wedding for June. I per-
> sonally do not like the way the traditional wedding cere-
> mony is built around the bride. It is not fair for Paul and
> his family. We plan a church wedding. Can you suggest
> some ways that we could change the wedding ceremony
> to be fair to Paul and his parents and leave the ceremony
> dignified?**
>
> **Sylvia**

I have two main gripes about the traditional wedding
ceremony: (1) It is too expensive and (2) it is built around
the bride. (I have discussed the expense problem.) I object
to both patriarchicalism (the male is superior) and matriarchicalism (the female is superior). With the wedding built
around the bride, we have an example of matriarchicalism.
I'd like to suggest a movement against this part of the
traditional wedding ceremony.

Let us put the reply to Sylvia's question in perspective
by first describing the traditional ceremony and then repeating it with the necessary changes to be fair to Paul
and his family. What formal organization do you see at
traditional church wedding ceremonies? It is somewhat
as follows. The people begin to gather at the church. There
is quiet preceremony (prenuptial) organ or piano music.
The ushers seat the women. The men tag along behind
like frightened puppy dogs. After the groom's parents are
seated in the right aisle, the most important parent, the
bride's mother, is seated last, at the most honorable time
and in the most honorable place. After a vocal selection,

the organist begins the wedding march (processional). More often than not it is a selection from Wagner's opera *Lohengrin*. The people understand this march to be saying, "Here comes the bride"——the high note of this "shindig." The clergyman, the groom, and the best man appear from somewhere at the front of the church auditorium. They can come through a small door, the window, or a hole in the wall, or just any place; it doesn't make much difference. You see, the groom is not important. Since you can't have a wedding without him, you have to sneak him in somewhere. Then, down the left aisle come some sweet little girls carrying flowers. Then follow some sweet big girls clad in beautiful colored dresses. Finally the big, important—the momentous—occasion arrives. As the left rear foyer door opens and in answer to the call of the organ, here really comes the bride on the arm of her father. All eyes are glued on the bride. Once at the altar, the clergyman inquires, "Who gives this woman to be married?" The father replies, "I do," and is seated beside his wife. Since the groom is so insignificant, there is no reason to present him to the bride. From this point on, the double-ring ceremony is a beautifully balanced ritual.

Now, Sylvia, let us repeat this as it ought to be, with a balanced ceremony planned around *both bride and groom*. During the quiet preceremony music, young men ushers seat the women and young women ushers seat the men in orderly dignity. Let us assume a church with two middle aisles. There would be two wedding processions. The parents of the bride and groom would not be seated but would be a natural part of the two processions. When the organist begins the wedding march (the wedding march from Wagner's *Lohengrin* could not be used since *this* ceremony is saying, "Here comes the *wedding party*"), the clergyman stands at the altar facing the audience. The two wedding processions begin. The two foyer doors back of each center aisle open, and down the left aisle march slowly some sweet little girls, while some sweet little boys slowly march down the right aisle, in balanced order. Next follow some sweet big girls clad in beautiful colored dresses down the left aisle and some handsome big boys in a balanced order down the right aisle. Next there comes through the left foyer door the bride between, and holding to the arms of, her mother and father. At the same time the groom comes through right foyer door between, and holding the arms of, his mother and father. The two meet at the altar, facing the clergyman. He says, "Who gives this woman to be married?" Her parents say in unison, "We do." Then the clergyman says, "Who gives this man to be married?" His parents say in unison, "We do." At this point the clergyman brings the bride and groom together in the center of the altar and unites their hands. The bride's maid and best man move into normal positions. The parents may be seated near the front or they may just stand aside and be a part of the total ceremony. I personally prefer the latter. From this point on, the beautiful, balanced double-ring ceremony continues normally.

There are several advantages of this balanced ceremony. The bride and groom are symbolically equal. The parents of the bride and the parents of the groom are symbolically equal. The bride and men and women in the ceremony symbolically are equals. There is no extra expense involved. The audience will take notice and be pleased at the balanced beauty and dignity of such a ceremony. If a church has only one center aisle, both processions would enter that aisle, one after the other. If the mother or father of either is not living, a near relative could stand in that person's place.

I challenge young people to consider this plan for a wedding ceremony. It involves only a little organization, but the meaning of the wedding, its spiritual interpretation, and its value will be long cherished and remembered. A well-planned wedding should help set an example for a happy marriage of interdependence and mutual self-giving.

WHAT ABOUT A MARRIAGE WITHOUT A LICENSE OR A WEDDING CEREMONY?

Dora wrote me the following letter, inquiring about the wisdom of a "common-law marriage," that is, a marriage in which a man and woman begin living together as husband and wife without buying a wedding license or having any kind of wedding ceremony, either public or private.

> **I have been dating this boy for several months. We have talked about by-passing a marriage license and any type of marriage ceremony and just simply begin to live together as husband and wife. He will be transferred from the factory here to another state in a few months. We could begin living together at that time. We are church members, and we have our own religious ideas. We want our marriage to be successful. We want some children, but we like to be independent and do our own thinking. Why should everybody go through the silly routines of buying a license and the equally silly and expensive wedding ceremony?**

I like to be objective and give other people the right to do independent thinking, but I cannot approve of common-law marriage. It is basically antisocial; that is, one who advocates it is announcing, "I'll live my own life the way I want to and everybody else can go 'jump in the lake.'" Suppose for a moment that we universalized Dora's idea and abolished all marriage licenses, marriage records, and marriage ceremonies; what would this mean? It would mean chaos, total social chaos. In order to have civilization, society must know *who is married to whom.* Even early primitive peoples recognized this. They did not have strict legal regulations with permanent marriage records in a county courthouse. But they require a marriage ceremony, and all the community was invited. These were major social occasions. Their real purpose was the need for making a marriage known by establishing it before witnesses so that through the years they would know who is married to whom. No society, past or present, has ever existed without some controls over human behavior. Controls over marriage and the family are basic to proper control of human behavior.

In spite of these facts, common-law marriages have been tolerated in our society, but they are now illegal in thirty-six states.

I note that Dora identifies herself with Christianity. The Scriptures call for followers of Christ to cooperate with community social organization, so long as it is not in conflict with basic Christian teachings. The last six of the Ten Commandments are social commandments.

Why does Dora want to keep her marriage so secret? Is she ashamed of her fiancé? Is she afraid of his values and lack of social and moral stability? Is she afraid that her marriage won't last? Is she looking for an easy way out if it doesn't work? Suppose she has children? Would she feel as responsible for caring for them as she would if she were legally married? Will she not be dependent on society (its schools, courts, churches, community youth organizations, etc.) to help her socialize her children? Suppose her husband gets tired of her, leaves, and claims that the relationship was never agreed upon as marriage; what could she do? It would be his word against hers. Suppose her husband became wealthy and then died; would she be able to inherit from him as his wife? And what about the legitimacy of their children? Would their children have inheritance rights? What will Dora do when her children grow up and ask about her marriage? How will they feel when they learn that all other children's parents are legally married and theirs are not?

I will never forget a distraught mother, age forty-five, who came to me privately with her problem. She was living in a common-law marriage. Everyone in the family was now an active church member. Her eighteen-year-old daughter had suspected the problem and was demanding to see her parents' marriage license. The burden of the mother's conversation was, "We regret that we did not have a legal marriage. It was a miserable mistake. What should we do now?" In the conversation she decided, in tears, that she had no alternative but to (1) ask God's forgiveness, (2) tell her daughter all, (3) ask her daughter's forgiveness, and

(4) see her pastor and a lawyer about the wisdom of planning a legal marriage immediately.

Is it possible that the real reason Dora objects to a marriage license and ceremony is that she is unsure of herself, unsure of her fiancé, radically self-centered, or really looks upon marriage as a tentative relationship?

I have stated earlier in this chapter that formal weddings can be expensive—too expensive. But would it not be wiser for a person who objects to the expense and formality of a wedding ceremony to buy a marriage license and have a small, inexpensive home wedding? The legal trend in our society is to do away with common-law marriages.

In life and in marriage, we must live in society. Any couple will live to rue the day that they enter a marriage that is not accepted by society.

A SUGGESTED MARRIAGE CEREMONY

Friends, we are gathered together in the sight of God and in the presence of this company to join together this man and this woman in holy matrimony. Commended by the apostle Paul to be honorable among all people, marriage is not to be entered into lightly or unadvisedly, but reverently and discreetly, and in the fear of God. Into this holy estate these two now come to be joined.

Marriage is God's first institution for the welfare of the race. From the beginning of time before the forbidden tree had yielded its forbidden fruit or the tempter had touched the world, God said that it was not good for man to be alone. He therefore made a help suitable for him and established the rite of marriage, while heavenly hosts witnessed the wonderful scene.

Originated in divine wisdom and goodness, designed to promote human happiness and holiness, the rite of marriage is the very foundation of home life and social order, and must so remain until the end of time. Sanctioned and honored by the presence and power of Jesus at the marriage in Cana of Galilee, it marked the beginning of His mighty works. Throughout the Bible marriage is pictured as being approved by God. And when the Holy Spirit, wishing to equip the Church with a fit metaphor, chose marriage as that metaphor, the holy rite received its highest tribute. So it is ordained that a man shall leave his father and his mother and cleave only to his wife, and they shall be one flesh, united in one hope, in one aim, and in one sentiment, until death do them part.

Who now gives this woman to be married to this man? (Father: "Her mother and I.") or (Father and Mother: "We do.")

If you, then, John and Mary, have freely and deliberately chosen one another as partner in this holy estate, and if you know of no just cause why you should not be thus united, you will please join your right hands.

John, will you take this woman to be your wedded wife, to live together after God's ordinance in the holy estate of matrimony? Will you love her, honor and keep her, both in sickness and health, in poverty and in wealth, keeping yourself only to her so long as you both shall live? (Groom: "I do.")

And Mary, will you take this man to be your wedded husband, to live together after God's ordinance in the holy estate of matrimony? Will you love him, honor and keep him, in sickness and in health, in poverty and in wealth, keeping yourself only to him so long as you both shall live? (Bride: "I do.")

Then you, John, shall repeat after me: I, John, take you, Mary, to be my wedded wife: to have and to hold from this day forward, for better or worse, for richer or poorer, in sickness and in health, in poverty or in wealth, to love and to cherish until death do us part, according to God's holy ordinance; and thereto I pledge you my vows.

And you, Mary, shall also repeat after me: I, Mary, take you, John, to be my wedded husband: to have and to hold from this day forward, for better or worse, for richer or poorer, in sickness and in health, in poverty or in wealth, to love and to cherish until death do us part, according to God's holy ordinance; and thereto I pledge you my vows.

From time immemorial the ring has been used to seal important covenants. When the race was young and parliaments yet unknown, the Seal of State was worn fixed upon a ring belonging to the reigning monarch, and its stamp on a document was the sole seal of imperial authority. From such impressive precedent the ring, the golden circle and the most prized of tokens, has come to its loftiest prestige in the symbolic office its use contributes to the marriage altar. Here, untarnishable material and unique form become a precious token of a pure and abiding love that will never tarnish and never have end. In like token, you have chosen to give each to the other a ring, thereby signifying your eternal love one for the other.

You, John, will repeat after me as you place this ring on your bride's hand: With this ring I thee wed, and with all my worldly goods I thee endow, in the name of the Father, and of the Son, and of the Holy Spirit. Amen.

And as you, Mary, place this ring on his hand, you shall repeat after me: With this ring I thee wed, and with all my worldly goods I thee endow, in the name of the Father, and of the Son, and of the Holy Spirit. Amen.

An additional symbol to the giving and receiving of rings in the marriage ceremony is the uniting of light.

Before us now are three candles; two are lighted,

but the third, which is larger than a combination of the two, remains still unused. John and Mary, you see represented here before you both your past, your present, and your future. You are here today extinguishing a part of yourself to build a larger and brighter self in the union with your life's partner. You will each, therefore, take a candle, and from its flame together you will light the larger candle, symbolizing that your lives from this point on have been joined into a unity that will give light and happiness to you both. (Both light the third candle.)

Let us pray. (The prayer will vary from one clergyman to another.)

"What God has joined together, let not man put asunder." Forasmuch then, as John and Mary have united themselves in holy wedlock, and have testified to the same before God and those assembled here, sealing their vows with a ring and symbolizing them with the candles, by the authority invested in me as a Minister of the Gospel in the State of ......, I do declare them to be man and wife, in the name of the Father, and of the Son, and of the Holy Spirit. Amen.[1]

---

[1] This wedding ceremony, a compilation of several well-known ceremonies (including the Episcopal), is one often used by Charles C. Hobbs. Used by permission.

10

Planning the Honeymoon

HOW DOES A GIRL WHO IS AFRAID OF THE PHYSICAL SIDE OF MARRIAGE PREPARE FOR A HONEYMOON?

The following letter illustrates how a girl may fear sex in marriage:

> I am desperately in need of some help. I am engaged to be married in a few short months. I am nearly twenty-one years old and in good health. I have been excited about getting married, until recently. You see my wedding day is fast approaching, and my problem is that I am worried about my part of our honeymoon. Frankly, I am more than worried, I am scared. My fiance does not know how I feel. We agreed when we started going steady that sex belonged to marriage, but we have expressed our love in limited ways. My fiance has suggested twice recently that we must discuss sex before our marriage. I agreed, but keep putting it off. Will you please give me some help?

If a girl is in normal health, she should have no sexual problem in marriage. Some girls often needlessly worry over whether or not they are undersexed, will be capable of responses, and can enjoy normal sex life in marriage. God does not create undersexed women. He creates women. If there is a problem, it is generally mental and emotional. But let me hasten to say that most girls do not have any problem that cannot be corrected.

There are two basic things that cause a woman to be unable to enjoy normal sex life in marriage. The first is that she may think "sex is evil," except for reproduction. This attitude keeps a woman from responding normally with her husband. If a girl has this idea, where did she get it? She may get it from listening to tall tales from teenagers. She may get it from hearing her parents or pastor talk about the evils of sexual permissiveness. Note, they were not saying that sex is evil. They were saying that the misuse and abuse of sex is evil. Thus, as a growing child, some girls decide that sex is "kind of" evil. This idea is false and must be rejected.

The second reason for poor sex life in marriage is the lack of proper sex education before marriage. When a young bride goes into marriage knowing little about her own sexual nature (and sometimes her young husband knows even less) she may expect some unhappy experiences in marriage.

Often these two factors (the idea that sex is evil and a lack of sex education) work together. What can a girl (or boy) do to get rid of these fears? Read! Read what? I spent eleven years while a college professor teaching marriage and family classes, and while doing so, wrote a book to help young people prepare for the intimate marriage relationships.[1] It is written from a positive religious point of view, giving details about the Bible and sex and the techniques necessary for normal sexual adjustments in marriage.

If you are a girl with fears, you should secure a copy of the book and read it thoroughly. Then carefully reread chapters two, four, and five. Be sure to read Appendix II. After you have read it, give it to your fiancé to read. After he has read it, both of you should read it together. Stop often to discuss various ideas to be sure you understand what is said and that you understand each other's ideas. This should be done several weeks before your marriage. If after reading the book, you have further questions, talk to your pastor or some other qualified marriage counselor.

---

[1] *Sexual Happiness in Marriage* (Grand Rapids: Zondervan Publishing House, 1967), 158 pages.

When you go to your family doctor for a pelvic examination thirty days before your marriage, feel free to ask him any question that you still wonder about. A girl will not be able to rid herself of all her fears. Actually, almost all young women (and men) go into their marriage with some degree of wonder, shyness, and apprehension. If they follow the suggested approach, it should reduce fears to the lowest possible level and enable them to move on into marriage and the honeymoon with confidence and success.

Young people should avoid two extremes. At one extreme is the idea that "sex is everything; nothing else in life is worthwhile." This is a false and deadly idea. Your life will be sad if you follow it. At the other extreme is the idea that "sex is nothing; it is unimportant and insignificant." This is a false and deadly idea. Your life will be sad if you follow it. The truth lies between these two extremes.

SHOULD EVERY FIRST MARRIAGE BE FOLLOWED BY A HONEYMOON?

Mary raises the question of the importance of a honeymoon in the following letter.

> Mike and I plan to be married in June. Our families, and therefore both of us, have to be careful in our financial planning in order to survive in today's world of rising prices. Our questions to you are, "Do you think a honeymoon worth the expense involved when a couple is short on money? If so will you give us some suggestions on planning our honeymoon?"

Yes indeed, every first marriage ought to be followed by a honeymoon! Historically, some type of wedding ceremony has been universal, but the honeymoon is largely a social development of the twentieth-century Western world, and one of its finest. Marriage, in the plan of the Creator, is a one-time experience, a most significant event in life. The lingering memories of a happy honeymoon will bless one's life across the years. Plan it well!

The present cost of a motel room per night, for two

people and one bed is approximately $25.00 to $30.00. Food may cost $20.00 to $25.00 per day for two people. If you traveled in your car 300 miles at 25¢ per mile, your expense would be about $75.00 per day. Assuming a little extra for miscellaneous expenses, a seven-day, six-night honeymoon would cost $500.00 to $600.00. Or a five-day, four-night honeymoon would cost $300.00 to $400.00. I strongly recommend that you cut out some of the wedding expense and plan a honeymoon. For example, my research shows that an average 1980 wedding reception costs $700.00. Why not omit the formal wedding reception as suggested in an earlier chapter and have an informal reception by having the wedding party form a line in the church foyer immediately after the wedding ceremony and greet the people as they leave the church auditorium? Then use this money saved for a honeymoon. For years, I have studied young couples who did not have a honeymoon or had a short one involving only one night, and they all agree that if they had it to do over again they would cut expenses somewhere else, or even borrow the money in order to have a honeymoon of reasonable length.

The honeymoon should involve a minimum of four days and three nights to a maximum of ten days and nine nights. Seven days and six nights is ideal. I do not recommend a three-and-one-half-month trip to Europe, even for the wealthy. That trip should be at the first or some following anniversary. The honeymoon should start immediately after the wedding ceremony. A honeymoon postponed for six months is not a honeymoon.

The honeymoon should not be planned around a business trip or visits to relatives and friends. It should not involve extensive tiring travel, a busy schedule of work, or responsibility of any kind. It should involve complete isolation and privacy some fifty or more miles away from home. The place of your honeymoon probably should not be revealed to anyone. Call home the next morning to notify relatives where you can be found in case of an emergency. Allow your honeymoon to be a time of complete relaxation, when you replace fatigue, tension, and fear with mutuality, tenderness, kindness, and patience.

I recommend that you take two books with you on your honeymoon. First, the Bible! On the first night you should each read aloud, one after the other, a specific Bible passage you have selected in advance. Then both should audibly lead in prayer one after the other in simple, sincere language, asking for God's leadership in your lives together. This is a humble, serious period, and rightly so. This period should be followed by an atmosphere of happiness, laughter, and joyful delight.

I wonder if any reader can guess what the second book would be? Yes, you guessed it! A copy of my book *Sexual Happiness in Marriage* (Zondervan, 1967). To reread this book together sometime during the honeymoon should help to further develop a two-way mutual understanding and appreciation of your "one-flesh" marriage relationship.

Your first sexual experiences are a major and central part of your honeymoon. However, you should not expect to accomplish too much sexually in a short period of four to seven days. Young people often dream about perfect sexual fulfillment on their wedding night, but this seldom happens. First experiences are often unsatisfactory, yet this is no cause for alarm. Good sexual adjustment in marriage often takes weeks, sometimes months, or longer. It is a process of understanding and growth. Couples continue to discover increased sexual happiness after ten or even twenty years of married life.

Although it is significant in your honeymoon, sex should not be the only concern during those happy days. You will want relaxed fellowship, walks hand-in-hand through scenic places in the mountains or at the seashore, long personal conversations, further planning and crystallizing of your dreams and ambitions for your total life together.

Yes, *every first marriage should be followed by a honeymoon.*

Bibliography

The following books written from a general Christian viewpoint are recommended reading in the area of courtship from puberty to marriage. They will be welcome reading in family, church, or community libraries.

I. GENERAL MARRIAGE AND FAMILY BOOKS THAT DISCUSS COURTSHIP IN DETAIL.

Bowman, Henry A. *Marriage for Moderns,* 6th ed. New York: McGraw-Hill, 1970.

Landis, Judson A., and Landis, Mary G. *Building a Successful Marriage,* 6th ed. Englewood Cliffs, New Jersey: Prentice-Hall, 1972.

Popenoe, Paul. *Marriage Is What You Make It.* New York: Macmillan, 1950.

II. SPECIFIC BOOKS ON THE SUBJECT OF COURTSHIP.

Duvall, Evelyn Millis. *The Art of Dating.* New York: Association Press, 1969.

Mace, David R. *Youth Considers Marriage.* Camden, New Jersey: Thomas Nelson and Sons, 1966.

McGinnis, Tom. *A Girl's Guide to Dating and Going Steady.* Garden City, New York: Doubleday and Company, 1968.

Riess, Walter. *For You, Teen-ager in Love.* St. Louis: Concordia Publishing House, 1960.

Shedd, Charles W. *Promises to Peter.* Waco, Texas: Word Books, 1970.

———. *Letters to Karen.* Nashville, Tennessee: Abingdon Press, 1965.

III. GENERAL BOOKS RELATED TO COURTSHIP AND SEX EDUCATION.

Crawford, Kenneth, and Simmons, Paul D. *Growing Up With Sex*. Nashville, Tennessee: Broadman Press, 1973.

Duvall, Evelyn Millis. *Love and the Facts of Life*. New York: Association Press, 1963.

————. *Why Wait Till Marriage?* New York: Association Press, 1965.

Fields, W. J., ed. *Life Can Be Sexual*. St. Louis: Concordia Publishing House, 1968.

Fitch, William. *Christian Perspectives on Sex and Marriage*. Grand Rapids, Michigan: Wm. B. Eerdmans Publishing Company, 1971.

Miles, Herbert J. *Sexual Happiness in Marriage*. Grand Rapids, Michigan: Zondervan Publishing House, 1967.

————. *Sexual Understanding Before Marriage*. Grand Rapids, Michigan: Zondervan Publishing House, 1971.

Vincent, M O. *God, Sex, and You*. Philadelphia: Lippincott Company, 1971.

Shedd, Charles W. *The Stork Is Dead*. Waco, Texas: Word Books, 1968.